SHAKER HERITAGE GUIDEBOOK

SHAKER HERITAGE GUIDEBOOK

Exploring the Historic Sites, Museums & Collections

STUART MURRAY

WHERE TO GO • WHAT TO SEE • HOW TO GET THERE

This information in this book was supplied in part by the sites themselves and is subject to change without notice. Before making final plans or reservations you may wish to call ahead to verify information. The author and publisher make no representation that this book is absolutely accurate or complete. Errors and omissions, whether typographical, clerical or otherwise may sometimes occur herein. Specific words may vary in spelling or usage depending on the site.

First Edition, January, 1994
Text Copyright © 1994 by Stuart Murray
Cover Design © 1994 Golden Hill Press

Library of Congress Catalogue Card Number 93-079992
ISBN 0961487666

Published in the United States of America by Golden Hill Press, Inc., Spencertown, New York.

The book was set in Sabon by Kath Moran of North Wing Studios, Stuart, Florida. Cover and book design by Rich Kraham of Design Unit, Chatham, New York. Word Processing by Maria Iglesias-Baxter, Chatham Answering Service. Copy editing by Judith Hoover.

Front Cover: Interior at Hancock Shaker Village, Hancock, Massachusetts. Photo: Paul Rocheleau.

Back Cover: Shaker Boxes at Shaker Museum and Library, Old Chatham, New York; Shakers at Mount Lebanon, New York; Bell at Sabbathday Lake, Maine; Outline of Hancock Shaker Village.

To the Gerritys—Jude, Rob,

Alexa, and Gretchen—in whose

house this book came to be.

FOREWORD

Our Still Small Voice

In 1961 our Community began publishing *The Shaker Quarterly.* The first article to appear was entitled, "Our Still Small Voice." Over the past thirty-two years there have been many changes wrought upon us. In the eyes of the World our voice might seem to have been almost silenced in point of our numbers. It seems most appropriate to us to quote from that long ago article:

> "Shakerism is not dead, nor will it soon be. We believe confidently that neither truth nor good can ever die. Since even our critics seem still to find something of these virtues in the movement, we feel that the end for which many have waited so long is not yet at hand. We are, however, quite ready to give over the movement itself into God's hands."

This guidebook has been well researched and offers to any student of Shakerism clear, concise information for locating and visiting this Community and former Shaker sites. In these places we hold dear to our hearts, so many consecrated souls labored to give their hands to work and their hearts to God. From what physically remains at these sites we hope that you will sense the spirit that has guided us and our forebears.

We pray as you begin your own journey you will come to more fully comprehend the Shaker story and the truths on which Shakerism has rested for over two hundred years. It is in this spirit that we raise this our still small voice.

THE SABBATHDAY LAKE SHAKERS

PREFACE

While the Shaker faith and way of life lives on today in the work and worship of the Believers in Sabbathday Lake, Maine, there is ever-growing interest in the Shaker heritage that left a legacy across the eastern United States.

More than ever, that interest is met with enthusiasm by those—professionals and volunteers—who are working to develop Shaker Village restorations, museum exhibits, collections, and scholarly studies and who practice Shaker crafts, sing their songs, and celebrate their way of life.

Even the most obscure Shaker historical site has people devoted to its legacy. Though there might be nothing left of a Shaker site, there is certain to be someone busy researching, collecting, at times sleuthing to find out what was built and how the Shakers lived there. Through the work of these people a dynamic network once again reunites the far-flung system of Shaker settlements.

In those who are busy with this legacy, affection for the Shakers mingles with profound respect. In that spirit, this book is offered, that it might honor America's Shaker heritage.

Stuart Murray
Chatham Center, New York

ACKNOWLEDGEMENTS

A large and dynamic network of persons interested in America's Shaker heritage contributed to this book, every one of them essential for its accuracy and integrity.

At each historical site and each collection, someone gave conscientious and intelligent assistance to our work. We hope that those who are not mentioned here will accept our deepest thanks for the help they gave.

In virtually every case, our requests were met with kindness and helpfulness, a testimony to how much people care about the Shaker legacy. Our only regret is that this book no more than touches on the wealth of knowledge and resources regarding the Shaker heritage.

The advice of the Sabbathday Lake Believers was central to our efforts, especially the contribution of Brother Arnold Hadd.

The staffs at Hancock Shaker Village and the Old Chatham Shaker Museum and Library gave crucial assistance right at the outset of this project. At Hancock Shaker Village: June Sprigg, Elizabeth Fitzsimmons, Robert Meader, and Magda Gabor. At the Shaker Museum and Library, Old Chatham: Viki Sand, Jerry Grant, Virginia McEwen, Joan Baldwin, and Cary Marriott.

Likewise, we are deeply indebted to Thomas Donnelly at Mount Lebanon, Marcheta Sparrow of Pleasant Hill, Tommy Hines of South Union, Cynthia Hunt of Canterbury, Maggie Stier at Fruitlands, Janet Allen at Watervliet, New York, Carolyn Smith at Enfield, New Hampshire, and Catherine Winans at the Shaker Historical Museum, Shaker Heights, Ohio.

Experts in Shaker who helped us included Professor Gustav G. Nelson of the Berkshire Shaker Seminars of Berkshire Community College; Stephen Paterwic, President of the

Boston Area Shaker Study Group, who read the manuscript; David D. Newell, who contributed much material for Savoy; Mary Lue Warner of the Otterbein Homes; Fran Kramer of the Rochester Area Shaker Study Group; and John Martin Smith, Mary Allen, Richard Spence, Martha Boice and Dr. Dale Covington, all of the Western Shaker Study Group, and Bill Cullen of Florida's Osceola County Historical Society, who enhanced the Narcoossee chapter.

Other friends of the Shaker legacy who contributed include James Ballard, Jere DeWaters, and Paul Rocheleau, photographers. Thank you to those who contributed information for Enfield, Connecticut: Richard Steinert, former warden of the Enfield Minimum Security Prison; Anthony Secondo, President of the Enfield Historical Society; and Charles Cybulski Jr., owner of the South Family Dwelling and nearby Shaker buildings.

The following people also gave invaluable assistance: Mrs. Howard L. Smith of Livingston County Historical Society; Doris Hoot, Chief Curator, Genesee Country Museum; Meredith Marcinkewicz of the Shirley Historical Society; Michael Corsini, facilities administrator of the MCI Shirley Minimum/Pre-release prison; Marilyn O'Rourke of the New Canaan Historical Society; Fred B. Compton of the Golden Lamb; Mary Payne of the Warren County Historical Museum; Melba Hunt of Kettering-Moraine Museum; Stewart Welsh, Deputy Director of the Hamilton County Park District; Judith Elsdon of the American Museum in Britain; and Nancy and Griff Mangan of Alasa Farms.

Also, thanks to the many representatives of historical societies, libraries, museums, collections, and educational institutions who contributed to the book.

Thanks to book designers Kath Moran and Rich Kraham, who brought words and ideas to reality; to Judith Hoover for editorial advice; and to Maria Iglesias-Baxter for keyboarding that advice.

Also, special thanks to those at the Chatham Public Library, Chatham, New York, which as always showed thoughtfulness and kindness in assistance with research.

Finally, profound thanks to Publisher Mary Zander, who made an enormous effort to pull together the many strands of this book and thus contribute another yard to the living fabric that is America's Shaker Heritage.

Stuart Murray
Chatham Center, New York

USING THIS BOOK

1. Each site chapter is **headed** with the site's commonly used name, its spiritual name, its location, and the dates Shakers were active there.

2. The **next headings** note anything distinctive about the site and an at-a-glance listing of what services are available to the visitor: museums, exhibits, libraries, shops, tours, special programs or events, on-premises lodging or dining.

3. The **first text** describes the site, its present appearance and management, the number of buildings remaining, and perhaps enlarges on some distinctive aspect.

4. **Site History** gives a picture of its founding, and some history or some facts about its major buildings—a capsule view of its "story."

If the site itself does not provide its visitors with a **site map**, then a map or sketch is given to indicate present buildings or remains and their locations, or to mark where the site was.

UNION VILLAGE

"Wisdom's Paradise"
Lebanon, Ohio
1805-1912   **1.**

Museums & Shops

Special Programs & Guided Tours   **2.**

Gift Shops, Dining & Lodging

The remaining structures of the approximately sixty that once made up Union Village are two residences and a dairy wing that are part of the Otterbein United Methodist retirement homes. A fledgling Shaker museum in **3.** Marble Hall here has been operating since 1987. Most of the former Union Village's artifacts that belong to Otterbein are on loan to the Warren County Historical Society Museum nearby. Also in Lebanon is the Golden Lamb, an historic inn which houses a Shaker collection.

History of the Site
In the year 1805, three Shaker missionaries from Mount Lebanon proselytized in southwestern Ohio and found fertile soil. They were well met by New Light Presbyterians who were reacting against the Calvinism of their regional synod and attracted by the Shaker message.

4. Soon after arriving in the area, the missionaries had their first converts, at a place called Turtle Creek, in Warren County. The community known as Union Village was established there in 1805. Laying the foundation for a community patterned after Mount Lebanon, the Shaker missionaries lived in a log cabin while the land was cleared,

185

4.

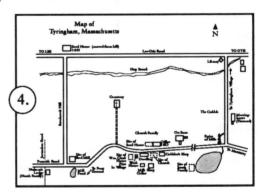

Map of
Tyringham, Massachusetts

5. **Planning Your Visit** notes guided or self-guided tours, exhibits, special programming, gift shops, accessibility to library, and so on.

6. **Tourist Information** is a summary, via text and symbols, of hours and days open, admission fee, handicapped accessibility, availability of restrooms, pets policy, and credit cards honored.

For some sites, this information is not applicable, since the site has no facilities or services. For these, consult "Resources" (next page). Addresses are given there for the local history society, or the area's Shaker Study Group, or the Berkshire Shaker Seminars or for Shaker site historians. All these groups and individuals have hands-on and specialized knowledge of one or more of the sites and arrange tours from time to time.

7. A **directional map** and narrative **directions** show the visitor how to reach each site area.

8. **Who to contact for further site or tour information** is given in the form of names, addresses and telephone numbers. The same is supplied for dining and lodging information, if available.

Because the names of their buildings (e.g., Dwelling House, Sisters' Shop) and their locations on site (e.g., Church family, West family) are dictated by the Shakers' beliefs and organizational structure, we suggest that you first read the Shaker Story chapter for a better understanding of the sites themselves.

Resources

Berkshire Shaker Seminars
Berkshire Community College
1350 West Street
Pittsfield, Massachusetts 01201

Arranges seminars and tours of
different Shaker sites each year.

Boston Area Shaker Study Group
c/o Moriarity
25 Forest Avenue
Natick, Massachusetts 01760
(Harvard & Shirley, Massachusetts
sites)

Albany Area Shaker Study Group
Shaker Heritage Society
Meeting House
Albany-Shaker Road
Albany, New York 12211
(Watervliet, New York site)

**Rochester Area Shaker Study
Group**
c/o Alasa Farms
Box 185
Alton, New York 14413
(Sodus & Groveland, New York
site)

Western Area Shaker Study Group
c/o Boice
7712 Eagle Creek Drive
Dayton, Ohio 45459
(Ohio and Indiana sites)

South Union Area Study Group
PO Box 70
South Union, Kentucky 42283
(South Union, Kentucky site)

John Martin Smith
PO Box 686
Auburn, Indiana 46706
(Busro site)

David G. Newell
39 Steady Lane
Ashfield, Massachusetts 01330
(Savoy, Massachusetts site)

CONTENTS

I
THE SHAKER STORY

*A doorway in the Centre Family Dwelling
at the restored Shaker Village of Pleasant
Hill at Harrodsburg, Kentucky. Courtesy
Shaker Village of Pleasant Hill.*

THE SHAKER STORY

The Shakers were the largest and most successful utopian movement in the United States, but their story begins in Manchester, England, in the mid-1700s.

The Shaker founders were a small group of English religious dissidents who had adopted the ritual practice of shaking, shouting, dancing, whirling, and "singing in tongues." Their wild dancing and jerking were indications of being possessed by spirits, a state they believed was a sacred experience.

These "Shaking Quakers" came to be led by a dynamic young woman named Ann Lee, who was born in 1736. Ann Lee and her little group were persecuted for their extreme behavior—attacked by mobs who considered them troublemakers and practitioners of witchcraft.

More than one Shaking Quaker, or "Shaker," was imprisoned for disturbing the peace, especially for desecrating the Sabbath by interrupting church services and exhorting congregations to change their sinful ways. During one such imprisonment, Ann Lee experienced what Shakers believe was the divine revelation that set her apart and made her their rightful leader. This revelation, she said, included celibacy, because "no soul could follow Christ in regeneration while living in the works of generation."

The biblical injunction "in the world, but not of the world" was also a cornerstone of the new faith. Calling themselves "Believers," the Shakers referred to everyone else as "the world" and resolved to live separately in their own communities.

Ann Lee's followers considered her to be wholly imbued with the spirit of Christ and named her the "Elect Lady" and "Mother of Zion." (The term "Zion" refers to the land of divinely chosen people.) Known to the Shakers as "Mother Ann," she eventually had a vision that inspired her to lead a portion of her followers to the New World, there to build a "millennial church"—the theological "millennium" being a period of one thousand years during which Satan would be bound and Christ would reign on earth.

To America

With her devoted brother, William, and six other followers, Ann Lee set out in 1774 for the British colony of New York, a difficult sea voyage on an old ship called *Mariah*.

The ship's crew despised and cursed the Shakers for their proselytizing, raucous singing, and wild dancing. The captain at one point even threatened to throw them overboard if they did not stop. Then, according to Shaker tradition, a brutal storm struck, threatening the ship.

The crew and Shakers labored to pump out the hold, but a loose plank in the hull had sprung a leak that could not be stanched. Mother Ann assured the despairing captain that the Lord would protect the ship as long as she and her disciples were aboard. Suddenly a rogue wave slammed against the *Mariah*, forcing the plank back into place so that the vessel stopped taking on water and was saved.

The New World

Within two years after arriving in New York, the Shakers had moved north, up the Hudson River to Albany. In a wilderness area called Niskayuna (or Watervliet by the Dutch), they built a rough log home and cleared some land for growing food.

By 1780, the Shakers had resumed their public testimony and began to preach the doctrines of celibacy, pacifism, and renouncing the ways of the flesh and the world. Led by Mother Ann, they traveled through the upper Hudson Valley and into Massachusetts, preaching to church groups and families.

The outbreak of the Revolution earned them hostility, for they were both English and pacifists. Accused of sedition and suspected of being a Loyalist, Ann Lee was arrested in the summer of 1780 and imprisoned until December. Other Shakers also were jailed, but for shorter periods. As the war began to ebb to its close, however, they were released and eventually left alone as harmless.

Setting the example for generations of Believers to come, the Shakers continued the hard work of draining their marshy Niskayuna farmland and making it productive. They also improved the house and at the same time began to harvest the fruits of their missionary work, as interested persons sought them out at Niskayuna.

The Missionary Journeys

The group began to grow, their missionaries traveling around the region, mostly into western New England. A "New Light" revivalist movement in the region helped increase conversions. Centered a day's ride to the east in New Lebanon, New York, New Lighters were for the most part Protestant separatists seeking more spiritual fulfillment than they had found in their former churches.

The "Millennial Praises," published in 1813 by the Shakers, described these early days in a hymn:

Near Albany they settled,   *At length a gentle whisper,*
And waited for a while,   *The tidings did convey,*
Until a mighty shaking   *And many flock'd to Mother,*
Made all the desert smile.   *To learn the living way.*

The year 1780 is considered by Shakers as the actual "opening" of their ministry in America. May 19 was the day of the first public testimony, known as the "Dark Day," when the sun did not shine in the region. The overshadowing, caused by smoke from forest fires consuming huge tracts in Quebec, was a sign to the Shakers that nothing ever would be as it had been, for their message was taking hold in the New World. This famous dark day touched off revivals all over New England and New York.

Ann and William Lee had been joined as leaders of the Shakers by James Whittaker, an English disciple. By 1780, they added the New Light Baptist minister Joseph Meacham, who was leading a congregation in New Lebanon, New York. Many of Meacham's own New Light friends and family near his home in Enfield, Connecticut eagerly took to Shaker teachings, and within a few years there were hundreds of converts in the Northeast.

In the early 1780s Mother Ann and the leaders carried out a series of missionary journeys throughout Massachusetts, Rhode Island, and Connecticut. This pilgrimage reaped a bounty of devoted new converts. It also earned lasting enmity from many of those whose friends and relations joined the Shakers. Mother Ann and her followers frequently were attacked and beaten by mobs. Despite opposition, they continued their missionary work.

At last, in September of 1783, they wearily returned to Niskayuna. Worn by missionary toil, beatings and sufferings, William Lee died in less than a year, and Mother Ann, soon after, on September 8, 1784. It was just ten years since her arrival in America, but her work was done. She had established the church that would come to be known as the United Society of Believers in Christ's Second Appearing.

Organizing the Millennial Church

Mother Ann was succeeded by James Whittaker, who led the Shakers until his death in 1786. It was Whittaker's successor and fellow preacher, Joseph Meacham, who truly organized

Shaker leaders at Canterbury ca. 1875. From left to right: James Kaime, Abraham Perkins, Benjamin Smith and Elder Henry C. Blinn.

the growing number of faithful who wished to live their lives according to the teachings laid out by Mother Ann. Shakers believed Meacham had been ordained by the hand of Mother Ann, who called him "the wisest man that has been born of a woman for six hundred years" and who predicted he would be her successor.

Mother Ann's doctrines of celibacy and living "in the world but not of the world" were very basic, more an outline rather than a strict plan of building. Meacham built on that basis, shaping the development of the United Society.

Well-versed in biblical tradition, "Father" Joseph created a threefold society of "courts" or families—a structure that changed and evolved throughout the next century. Broadly described, Meacham's organization was as follows: "Church" Family was formed from the most experienced and most faithful Shakers. Its leading aspect or "First" Family usually took responsibility for spiritual matters and internal administration in the community. The central meetinghouse was in its care, and the leading elders and eldresses were part of the First Family household.

The Second Family was mostly young adults who were less spiritually advanced but were devoted enough to offer hard physical labor on behalf of the community. It was involved with producing food and goods for the community's consumption or for sale to the world. These younger Believers were to develop spiritually as they worked, and at the same time they were the economic strength of the community.

The Third Family was mainly the elderly and children, along with a number of dynamic workers whose task was to conduct business with the world, including meeting persons interested in learning more about (and possibly joining) the Shakers. It was also called the "Office" Family. This family cared for the community's children, who attended school half the year, usually one in the community and run by the Shakers. The other half of the year the children worked full time in shops and fields, learning trades, handiwork, and household skills.

As the Shakers became more numerous, they developed and revised Meacham's structure. The Shaker village was organized so that each family lived and dined in its own dwelling and had its own offices and workshops.

Generally, a family's dwelling had a meeting room for its gatherings. The village usually had one main meetinghouse where the entire community came for Meeting on Sundays. Private Meetings were held in the morning, and in the after-

Shaker sisters in the Church Family kitchen at Mount Lebanon. From Leslie's Popular Monthly, XX, (December, 1885), No. 6.

noon the general public was permitted to attend Meeting.

The various families were also referred to according to their location in the layout of the community, with names such as Center, North, East, South, or West.

The scattered Shaker villages were organized into regional "bishoprics," with bishops and ministers sent out by appointment of the Central Ministry at New Lebanon. Most villages were established with the first leaders being sent from New Lebanon. Later the villages were led by local members who matured into positions of responsibility.

The Covenant

It was not until 1795 that the first written covenants were signed by Shakers, but in the early stages the Believers entered into an oral agreement to "stand as one joint community" for "the mutual support and benefit of each other."

The members gave all they had to the society, to be held in common, in equal shares. The communistic foundation of the Shakers was established at the outset, the members entering freely into the covenant for the sake of spiritual growth, both as individuals and as a group.

Though there were clear rules, the Shakers at first left much interpretation of how to practice their faith up to the individual Believer. To accommodate growth, however, there had to be a structure, and the instruction of Joseph Meacham gave form to faith. Yet, it remained to the Believer to look within and decide how best to contribute, each in his or her own way, to the spiritual and physical well-being of the whole.

By the mid-19th century, the Shaker doctrine had been more formalized. Although the teachings were originally intended to be simple and practical, as the years passed regulations for personal conduct became increasingly codified—to the point that for one brief period around 1845 there came to be a prescribed manner of kneeling, of praying, of working and of behaving.

During their first decades, Shakers performed ritual dancing in close order, but also separated according to gender. In later years ritual dancing no longer was practiced in Shaker worship; instead, brethren and sisters sat facing one another, divided by an aisle, singing and praying and "offering testimony" when moved to do so.

The practice of celibacy and the separation of the sexes became refined to the extent that there were separate doors for men and women. A brother was not to pass a sister on the stairs, nor were they permitted to speak together without a third Shaker present as chaperone. On the other hand, special family meetings were organized in which small groups of brethren and sisters would gather for a sociable hour, singing and conversing. In this way some of the natural tension that could arise from the strict segregation could be relieved.

Equality of men and women was a Shaker precept right from the start. Equality of race also was fundamental, and there are stories of Shakers purchasing slaves in order to free them. When Shaker missionaries preached at Philadelphia in 1846, a group of blacks joined the order and moved to

Watervliet for a while. Among these was Mother Rebecca Johnson, an itinerant preacher. After leaving the Shakers and returning to her home city, she on her own founded the Philadelphia community, which was half white and half black.

Across Half a Continent

Between 1780 and 1815 the Shakers spread their gospel rapidly. Whole families joined, accepting the communal ownership of property and the raising of children by the group. One of Joseph Meacham's first acts had been to name Lucy Wright as head of the order "in the female line." "Mother" Lucy was one of the most important leaders, guiding the Believers for twenty-five years and authorizing the westward expansion early in the 19th century.

Development of Shakerdom roughly followed that of the United States. New Yorkers and New Englanders established the first Shaker villages in the late 1700s, with communities at Watervliet, New York, in 1776 (the first settlement and home of Mother Ann), and New Lebanon, New York, in 1787, Hancock, Massachusetts, and Enfield, Connecticut, in 1790, and Harvard, Massachusetts, in 1791.

Tyringham, Massachusetts, and Canterbury, New Hampshire, were founded in 1792. Three societies got underway in 1793: Alfred, Maine; Enfield, New Hampshire; and Shirley, Massachusetts. In 1794, Sabbathday Lake, Maine, was the last village founded in the 18th century, and in 1808 nearby Gorham, Maine, was the last eastern seaboard village to be established.

At that time, three western communities were being settled, founded by Shaker missionaries who had walked most of the way to the Ohio Valley beyond the Appalachians. Settlements were established in southwestern Ohio at Union Village in 1805 and Watervliet in 1806 and in the heart of Kentucky at Pleasant Hill in 1805 and South Union in 1807.

In 1807 Shaker pioneers founded a village at Busro, Indiana, on the Wabash River, at the edge of Indian country. (A sawmill on the Illinois side of the Wabash belonged to the Shakers, but all that remains is the foundation and some timbers.)

In Massachusetts, a community was attempted at Savoy in 1817. The next societies were formed at North Union, near Cleveland, in 1822; at White Water, in southwestern Ohio in 1822; and in 1826 at Sodus Bay on Lake Ontario in western New York. By 1836 the Sodus Bay community had been compelled to leave, mistakenly believing it stood in the path of canal construction. These Shakers moved en masse to Groveland, New York, some ninety miles to the southwest.

In 1895, Shakers from Watervliet, and Mount Lebanon (as New Lebanon was called after 1861), New York, developed a site at Narcoossee, Florida. Three years later Shakers from Union Village, Ohio, built at White Oak, Georgia. The latter lasted only into the earliest years of the 20th century (1902). "Olive Branch," the settlement in Florida, functioned until 1924.

The number of Believers reached a peak in the 1840s, when there were approximately 4,000 members living in eighteen long-lasting villages. Communities at Gorham, Busro, Savoy and Sodus Bay were short-lived, but a total of twenty-four Shaker communities had been planted across a thousand miles from East to West. Some communities, such as Mount Lebanon, had as many as 600 members; others, like Watervliet, Ohio, and Tyringham, Massachusetts, never had more than 100-150 Believers.

Mount Lebanon was the "Center of Union," the spiritual and administrative headquarters for all Shakerdom. In the Midwest, Union Village in Ohio was the administrative seat, subordinated to the Central Ministry in Mount Lebanon.

Shaker Quality

It was partly because of their resolute devotion to both community and faith that the Shakers became the most prosperous and best-known "intentional" religious community in

NORTHEAST

MIDWEST

THE SHAKER COMMUNITIES

1. Sabbathday Lake, Maine	1794-	
2. Gorham, Maine	1808-1819	
3. Alfred, Maine	1793-1931	
4. Canterbury, New Hampshire	1792-1992	
5. Enfield, New Hampshire	1793-1923	
6. Tyringham, Massachusetts	1792-1875	
7. Harvard, Massachusetts	1791-1918	
8. Shirley, Massachusetts	1793-1908	
9. Savoy, Massachusetts	1817-1821	
10. Hancock, Massachusetts	1790-1960	
11. Enfield, Connecticut	1790-1917	
12. New Canaan, Connecticut	1810-1812	
13. Mount Lebanon, New York	1787-1947	
14. Watervliet, New York	1776-1938	
15. Sodus Bay, New York	1826-1836	
16. Groveland, New York	1836-1892	
17. North Union, Ohio (Shaker Hts.)	1822-1889	
18. Union Village, Ohio (Lebanon)	1805-1912	
19. Watervliet, Ohio (Dayton)	1806-1900	
20. White.Water, Ohio	1822-1916	
21. West Union, Indiana (Busro)	1807-1827	
22. Pleasant Hill, Kentucky	1805-1910	
23. South Union, Kentucky	1807-1922	
24. White Oak, Georgia	1898-1902	
25. Narcoossee, Florida	1895-1924	

SOUTHEAST

Two Shaker inventions. A crushing mill (right) and a vacuum pan, used to reduce dried roots to powder, part of their herb processing. Harper's New Monthly Magazine, No. LXXXVI, July 1857.

the United States. The most significant reason for their success, however, was the quality of their work.

"Hands to work and hearts to God," Mother Ann had said, perhaps her most famous quote. As practical as they were devout, the first Shakers well knew how to reap a harvest and sell what they made. They were often as good at business as they were at invention. Many hands working in unity was also a key, requiring a common purpose and self-effacement for the sake of the group.

Shaker designs were recognizable, their handwork known and widely respected across America. Form was to follow function, an object's beauty to emanate from its efficiency and simplicity. Although there were occasional forays into ornate Victorian fashion in building and furniture, Shaker simplicity in design endured because it was a most basic tenet of the faith.

Also enduring was the Shaker reputation for quality in

manufacture and production. Shaker goods, from seeds to chairs to brooms, were sold everywhere. Each Shaker community was known regionally for some field of commercial expertise, whether for pharmacology and herbal remedies or for the silk industry and fine cloth, for broom-making or for a certain style of furniture.

In time, Shaker ingenuity created a number of important inventions, including the screw propeller, a rotary harrow, an automatic spring, a threshing machine, a turbine water wheel and the circular saw. There was even an industrial washing machine, which the Canterbury Shakers patented and sold to large institutions such as hospitals. In the mid-19th century the Shakers ran the country's largest packaged seed industry, their salesmen ranging up and down rivers from town to village to farm. During the 19th century and into the first decades of the 20th the Shakers were widely known for such items as table condiments, cider, maple syrup, and packaged herbs, all highly regarded because they had the name "Shaker" on the labels.

Shaker religious ceremonies held for the benefit of the public were invariably crowded affairs, attended by casual tourists and spiritual seekers alike. Though for the most part respected, the Shakers and their ways were often publicly ridiculed, and they still occasionally were hated by those whose loved ones had entered the order.

Closing Down Villages

Nineteenth-century industrialization and urbanization moved Americans West. Railroads were built, steam power and assembly-line manufacturing prevailed as the earthy, agrarian existence of the Shakers lost its appeal to a generation that was becoming less religious and more urbanized. The Shakers rapidly dwindled in number.

In a parallel development, by as early as 1850 the passionate spiritualism and physical trembling of the Shakers were no longer important parts of their worship. By the last decades of the century they were seldom experienced or even

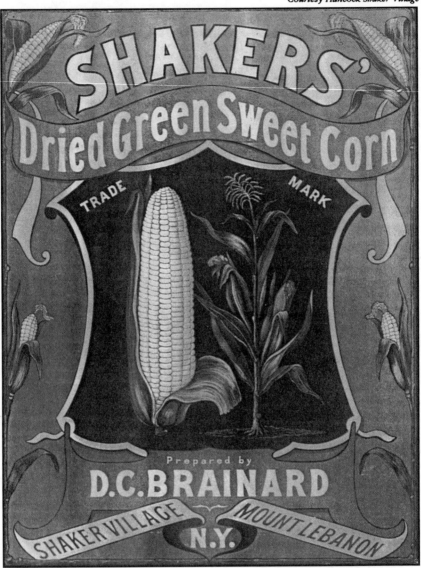

The Shakers were the first to offer seeds for sale in small paper envelopes; they were also the first to offer farmers the convenience of buying seed in large cloth bags for pasture crops. The Shaker name was by this time synonymous with honesty in business dealings, hard work, inventive genius and artistry.

desired. Work, however, remained a fundamental expression of faith.

As the world changed, the Shakers became increasingly involved with it, often speaking out publicly on current social issues. By the end of the 19th century leading Shakers were active in progressive affairs, lecturing impressively not only on the tenets of their faith, but also on feminism, suffrage, pacifism, and health. Some even began to vote.

More than ever, though, daily matters of survival economics and finance absorbed the attention of the leaders. The villages were deteriorating, and it was difficult or impossible to maintain them.

After the Civil War, although there was significant interest in Shakerism, there were few permanent converts, and Shaker membership often came to depend on the orphans and foster children taken in as wards. These children were entitled to choose whether to join or not when they came of age. Relatively few joined the Society, however, and by the last quarter of the 19th century the Shakers numbered no more than 900. When there were not enough Believers to care for buildings or run the workshops, employees and contractors were hired to do the work.

As the Believers became elderly, the villages were closed and sold off one by one and with much heartache. The survivors of each closed community were moved to others, sometimes to find themselves moving again as that community closed. In a few places the elderly were allowed by the new owners to live out their years in the dwelling houses that had been their lifelong homes. Around them, nursing homes and orphanages were established in their former buildings.

In 1947, the Shakers left Mount Lebanon, and in 1960 Hancock closed, leaving only Sabbathday Lake, Maine, and Canterbury, New Hampshire.

To raise much-needed funds, Shakers sold their personal furniture to the collectors who were beginning to take an interest in Shaker objects. This was painful, for it meant the

Orphan boys. Photographed by the Shakers at Watervliet before the turn of the century.

dissipation, bit by bit, of a heritage that had been built up over two centuries.

Shaker leaders of the past fifty years have felt it their duty to preserve the legacy, and their efforts have resulted in much being preserved for the public to see. In the past twenty-five years, historical societies and friends of Shakers have organized wherever a Shaker society existed and have worked to preserve that heritage in museums, restorations, and educational programs.

Shakers Today

The Shaker story is not told only in museums and restored villages, for it is not finished. At Sabbathday Lake, a group of eight Believers still puts hands to work and hearts to God, keeping the Shaker faith very much alive. (In 1992, Canterbury celebrated two hundred years as a living village, having one surviving sister, Ethel Hudson, still in residence. Sister Ethel passed away later that year, leaving Sabbathday Lake as the only remaining active Shaker village.)

Orphan girls. Photographed by the Shakers at Watervliet before the turn of the century.

As with other Shaker "sites," Sabbathday Lake has a museum and a number of buildings open to the public. And Sabbathday also has an active group of "Friends of the Shakers," who are concerned that not only the legacy but the way of life of the Believers be perpetuated.

The fundamental Shaker principles are observed at Sabbathday, with regular religious services to which interested persons are welcome. Here, more than anywhere else, visitors respect the Shaker way, as it lives on "in the world but not of the world."

Vassar College students demonstrate a Shaker dance at the Watervliet Meetinghouse.

Photo: Jere DeWaters

Sabbathday Lake as it looks today.

II
THE SITES

A family portrait of seven of the eight Shakers at Sabbathday Lake. Front row, (l-r), Sisters June Carpenter, Minnie Greene, Frances Carr, and Marie Burgess; rear (l-r), Brothers Arnold Hadd and Wayne Smith, and Sister Margaret Haskell. Absent from the photograph was Sister Ruth Nutter.

SABBATHDAY LAKE

"Chosen Land"
New Gloucester, Maine
Established 1794

> *Only Remaining Active Shaker Community*
> *Museum, Library, Exhibits*
> *Special Programs & Guided Tours*

Unique among all the Shaker sites, Sabbathday Lake is the only remaining living community of Believers.

Once considered the most remote and unimportant of Shaker Villages, little Sabbathday Lake has endured for almost two centuries, outlasting all the other Shaker communities. In that time it has become the repository of a world-renowned collection of Shaker material, which is available for viewing in its Library.

The Village today is a compact cluster of eighteen well-maintained buildings of the Church Family on 1,900 acres overlooking Sabbathday Lake. The eight Believers live in the 1883 Brick Dwelling with its forty-eight rooms, where they sleep, eat, and hold some of their worship services. The North Family, which lived over the town line in Poland, has no remaining buildings. A Shaker cemetery marks the site.

The Believers at Sabbathday Lake (the United Society of Shakers) are strongly supported by an active group of volunteers called "The Friends of the Shakers" This group helps in many ways, physically and materially. An extended "summer family" lives at Sabbathday Lake during the public season, Memorial Day to Columbus Day, when as many as twenty-

Photo: Jere DeWaters

Kitchen entry, 1987

five persons—including volunteer staff and hired help—gather for meals.

The Sabbathday Lake Shakers, following Shaker tradition, are generous in their charities and involved in community affairs, such as helping support a homeless shelter in Portland. They also take part in ecumenical interchange with other faiths and other spiritual seekers. They often are guest participants in events and programs based on America's Shaker tradition, leading songs and presenting the unvarnished truth of Shakerism to interested persons.

Sisters' Benches in the Winter Chapel, 1986.

The Publishing Role

The Sabbathday Lake Shakers have built up a lively publishing enterprise, producing publications that are essential for the student of the Shaker past and present: volumes of Shaker music; portfolios of "gift drawings"; scholarly studies of Shaker; cookbooks, children's books, and various catalogs.

Their elegant hardbound book, *Shakerism, Its Meaning and Message,* was first published by the order at Mount Lebanon in 1905. Written by Sisters Anna White and Leila S. Taylor, it is the definitive interpretation of the Shaker story up to that time as told by the Shakers.

One of Sabbathday's most important publications is *The Shaker Quarterly,* rich with history, art, architecture, and theology. Described as "a journal of scholarly investigation into Shaker," the *Quarterly* is produced and written by current Believers. Outside authors also are encouraged to submit articles for publication.

Courtesy the United Society of Shakers, Sabbathday Lake

The 1794 Meetinghouse, built by Moses Johnson, as were so many Shaker meetinghouses in the Northeast.

Sabbathday Lake Shaker Village, with the Visitors Center in the former Boys' Shop, second from right.

The Shaker Village at Sabbathday Lake in 1850. Joshua H. Bussell (1816-1900). Part of the collection of the Shaker Library at Sabbathday Lake.

History of the Site

Sabbathday Lake takes its name from a nearby body of water, so called because in the 1700s backwoodsmen would gather there on Sundays. One of the most outstanding Shakers from this community was Sister Aurelia Mace (1835-1910), who corresponded with Tolstoy and other luminaries of her time.

Sabbathday Lake was the eleventh society established. It remained small, so that over the years it played only a minor role in the United Society. At its peak in the early 19th century, it had no more than 150 Shakers.

Because they had few buildings to begin with, the Believers at Sabbathday Lake did not share the same overwhelming burden of larger Shaker villages—that of trying to maintain many empty buildings. Further, to avoid costly and futile maintenance, they razed dilapidated buildings that were unusable.

Consolidating with the Alfred Society when the latter closed in 1931 helped strengthen and solidify the Sabbathday Lake group. And while other societies became more worldly and changed their ways, the Maine Believers remained relatively conservative and secluded. Thus, when most surviving Shaker communities had—by the start of the 20th century—too few members to continue holding regular worship services and observation of traditional Shaker customs lapsed, Sabbathday Lake Believers continued to read the Shaker Covenant annually and to observe special days, such as Mother Ann's birthday on March 1 (or February 29 in leap years).

Shaker Library

Originally built as the Schoolhouse in 1880 to serve both Shaker and nearby children, the library represents a special achievement by the Sabbathday Shakers and their friends. Closed down in 1950, the Schoolhouse was bought by a neighbor and moved to his property in 1957. In 1986 Sabbathday Lake repurchased the building—by then dilapidated—and re-

Photo: Golden Hill Press

The Shaker Schoolhouse, restored and now the community library.

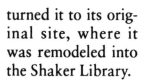

Ministry's Shop, 1839

turned it to its original site, where it was remodeled into the Shaker Library.

A large achievement for the little community, the library has one of America's finest collections of Shaker books, manuscripts, ephemera, biographical information, periodicals, photographs, and oral history recordings. There is a full-time librarian/archivist who is assisted by members of the Shaker community.

The Library also contains special collections related to radical religious sects and communal groups all over the world, many of which parallel the development of the Shakers. These include Freewill Baptists, Koreshan Unity, Southcottian, Swedenborgian, Hutterites, Zoar, Mormon, and Oneida.

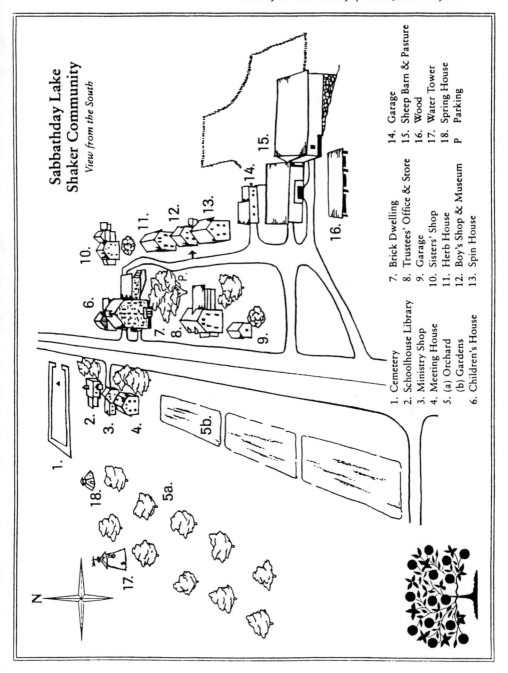

Sabbathday Lake Shaker Community
View from the South

1. Cemetery
2. Schoolhouse Library
3. Ministry Shop
4. Meeting House
5. (a) Orchard
   (b) Gardens
6. Children's House
7. Brick Dwelling
8. Trustees' Office & Store
9. Garage
10. Sisters' Shop
11. Herb House
12. Boy's Shop & Museum
13. Spin House
14. Garage
15. Sheep Barn & Pasture
16. Wood
17. Water Tower
18. Spring House
P. Parking

Planning Your Visit

Sabbathday Lake Believers maintain a delicate balance: preserving their privacy while still being open to visitors. The public is welcome to visit Sabbathday Lake from Memorial Day to Columbus Day, Monday through Saturday. The Museum and Gift Shop are open to the public at these times. A collection of Shaker furniture, tin- and woodenware, textiles, folk art, and early American tools and farm implements are on display in the Museum, which is located on the top two floors of the Meetinghouse. The Library is available, by appointment, Monday through Friday year-round. Those who wish to explore more of the Village must take a guided tour, entering some buildings and seeing all the others from outside. Visitors may not wander at will.

Guided Tours: Tour guides lead the groups through the 1794 Meetinghouse, 1839 Ministry's Shop and 1850 Boys' Shop. An "extended tour," offered only in July and August, also includes parts of the 1821 Sisters' Shop and 1816 Spin House.

The Shaker Store is housed in the 1816 Trustees' Office, which is also used to house invited guests of the community.

One of the most graceful structures is the 1903 Water Tank Tower, originally built to provide water for the Dwelling and now used to water the nearby orchard and gardens. Not far away is the 1878 Spring House, which still feeds the Laundry.

The 1824 Herb House is still in considerable use for drying herbs in the attic to supply the community's lively business in herbal products, sold in the store and by mail order.

Also still in use is the 1880 Ash House, for safe disposal of wood ashes from the stoves. The 1847 Stable and Ox Barn, originally separate buildings, were joined in the 1890s. The stable currently houses farm equipment and the community's flock of sheep, which are kept for their wool.

The oldest structure in the community is the Cart and Carriage Shed, a 1760s building put up by a colonist decades before the Shakers came to Sabbathday.

Public Meetings: The bell which once hung in the Alfred, Maine, Church Family Dwelling House is used here at Sabbathday Lake to mark the beginning of the Sunday summer worship services. It can be heard all over the community's 1,900 acres.

Not used in cold months, the large Meetinghouse is, in the summer, the site of the "Public Meetings," which are open to visitors. In these meetings, men and women sit apart, facing one another across an open aisle. The simple worship service opens with readings from the Bible and homilies. Guests take part in the singing of hymns that traditionally begin Shaker worship. The meeting is then opened to the offering of "testimony," and visitors, too, may speak if so moved. There is also spontaneous singing through the service.

SPECIAL PROGRAMS
Organized by the community, these include Shaker studies courses, public exhibits, and craft workshops.

Tourist Information

Museum, Shop and Store Hours: Memorial Day to Columbus Day, Monday through Saturday, 10 a.m.-4:30 p.m. Closed Sundays. Sabbathday Lake Village is open to the public during the same days and hours as the Museum.
Library Hours: Open year-round, Monday through Friday, 8:30 a.m.-4:30 p.m.— closed noon to 1 p.m. Appointments preferred.

For further site/tour information contact:

The United Society of Shakers
RR 1, Box 640
Poland Spring, Maine 04274
Tel: 207/926-4597

For lodging/dining information contact:

The Maine Publicity Bureau
Yarmouth Information Center
PO Box 1057
Yarmouth, Maine 04096
Tel: 207/846-0833

Access to Sabbathday Lake

DIRECTIONS: Sabbathday Lake is in the Town of New Gloucester, Cumberland County, on Route 26, 3 miles south of Poland Spring, 25 miles north of Portland. Take Exit 11 off the Maine Turnpike and go north on Route 26.

Admission Fee   Limited Handicapped Access   Restrooms   No Pets

No Credit Cards Accepted

33

*Elder Joseph Brackett, 1797-1882,
a prominent Gorham Shaker,
composed the famous song,
"Simple Gifts."*

GORHAM

"Union Branch"
Gorham, Maine
1808-1819

Claims "Simple Gifts" Composer

Shaker Gorham today consists of several buildings in what is now the Town of Gorham, a small village a few miles west of the Maine coast. These remaining Shaker buildings are all privately owned. They are the 1808 Dwelling, the Office, and a house thought to have been the house of Thomas Bangs, a founder of the Gorham Society. All three buildings are frame structures.

History of the Site

Although the first missionary work was begun in Gorham in 1784 and produced many enthusiastic Believers, they were still linked to the larger Alfred community in those early days. Finally, in 1807, fifty Shakers were organized or "gathered" into a community in Gorham—spiritually named "Union Branch"—taking up residence in what was then farmland owned by Believers Barnabas Bangs and Isaac Brackett, on Gray Road. The community remained there until 1819. In that year it was deemed more practical to move the Gorham Believers to New Gloucester.

At one time there were seven Shaker-owned structures in Gorham. After the Shakers left the site, two of the other original buildings were purchased and moved, and two of the original barns collapsed in the 1970s, leaving three buildings on the site.

A distinction of Gorham is its connection with the writer of a famous Shaker song. Joseph Brackett, son of Isaac Brackett of Gorham and eventually an elder in the Sabbathday Lake Community, composed "Simple Gifts" when living at Alfred.

Elder Joseph was said by the Shakers to be an excellent minister. He "possessed a remarkable and natural gift to sing by which he would often fill a whole assembly with the quickening power of God with his inspiration of song and his testimonies were often sharp and powerful as an edged sword and would often awaken sinners to repentance and lead them to make honest confession holding many who were on the brink of ruin."

Photo: Golden Hill Press

The former Brethren's Shop at Gorham.

Photo: Golden Hill Press

The former Trustees' Office, Gorham.

The words of Elder Joseph's famous song instruct, in a Shaker way, how to find spiritual humility:

'Tis the gift to be simple, 'tis the gift to be free,
'Tis the gift to come down where we ought to be,
And when we find ourselves in the place just right
'Twill be in the valley of love and delight.

When true simplicity is gained,
To bow and to bend we shan't be ashamed,
To turn, turn will be our delight
Till by turning, turning we come round right.

This song was discovered in a collection of Shaker music by composer Aaron Copland, who gave the old melody new fame when in 1944 he used it in the score of the Martha Graham ballet "Appalachian Spring."

Map: Golden Hill Press

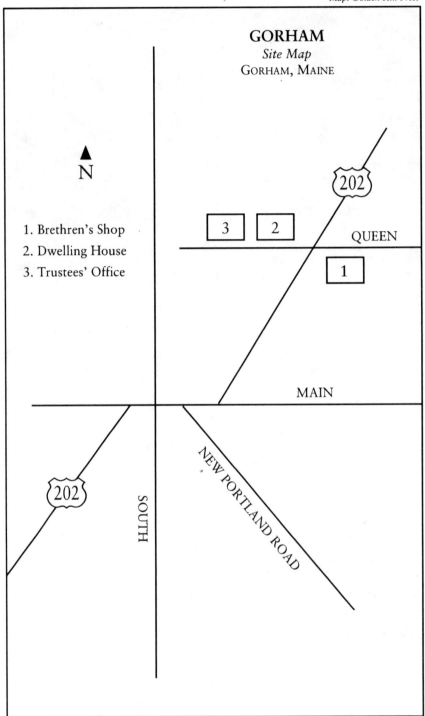

GORHAM
Site Map
GORHAM, MAINE

N

1. Brethren's Shop
2. Dwelling House
3. Trustees' Office

3   2

202

QUEEN

1

MAIN

NEW PORTLAND ROAD

202

SOUTH

Planning Your Visit

The remaining Shaker structures at Gorham can be seen only from the outside, as they are privately owned and there are at present no guided tours. Some site interpretation is available from the Shakers at Sabbathday Lake. The site map shows the location of the remaining Shaker structures. They are near the intersection of Route 202 (Gray Road) and Queen Street.

When you stand on Gray Road and face north, the house on the right is Shaker, and directly across on the northwest corner of Gray and Queen is a second; a third Shaker house is beyond, at the northwest corner of Queen and Libby Streets. Please respect the owners' privacy.

For further site/tour information contact:

Museum at Sabbathday Lake
The United Society of Shakers
RR 1, Box 640
Poland Spring, Maine 04274
Tel: 207/926-4597

For lodging/dining information contact:

Maine Publicity Bureau
Yarmouth Information Center
PO Box 1057
Yarmouth, Maine 04096
Tel: 207/846-0833

Access to Gorham

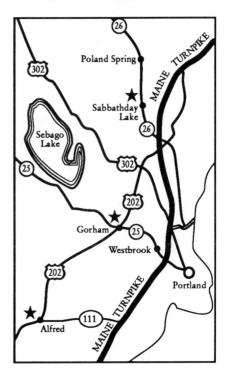

DIRECTIONS: Gorham is about 13 miles west of Portland; from I-95, take Exit 6A and follow northwest to Gorham. On Main Street, turn right and proceed to Gray Road (Route 202), third on left; turn left, go to Queen Street.

Eldress Fannie Casey stands in front of the Second Family Brethren's Shop and Dwelling House at Alfred, around the turn of the century.

ALFRED

"Holy Land"
Alfred, Maine
1793-1931

One of the Longest Lasting Communities

Alfred Village sits picturesquely on the side of a hill, overlooking the rolling farmland of southern Maine. Its seven former Shaker buildings are now privately owned.

The Alfred Shaker community is in the "South Coast" region of Maine, just northeast of Sanford and in the York County shire Town of Alfred. The Town of Alfred also is of considerable historical interest: the courthouse has the oldest court records in the U.S., dating back to 1635, and there are a number of houses from pre-Revolutionary days, including some that were occupied by Shakers.

A Shaker story tells of "Father" James Whittaker—one of the original Shaker party from England—and a few elders visiting Maine in 1785 and stopping at Alfred to visit.

"As they alighted from their horses, they stuck the willow withes used as whips into the ground," said the book *Shakerism* in 1905. "One hundred eleven years later, a visitor to the society describes the trees that had grown from these sticks as nearly three feet in diameter."

The willows growing around the seven remaining Shaker buildings of Alfred are the descendants of those same willow

Automobile and hay wagon before the Trustees' office, ca. 1910.

Second Meetinghouse and Ministry Shop at Alfred.

withes. The Village itself, which is southernmost of the three founded in Maine, has not been quite as enduring.

History of the Site

The Society at Alfred was organized in 1793 and became one of the longest-lasting communities, although by 1900 it had dwindled from 200 to thirty-nine Believers. For decades one of the most prosperous and self-sustaining Shaker communities —especially known for broom-making and the weaving of fine linen kerchiefs—Alfred was one of six remaining Shaker villages when it was sold in 1931.

Where once were three Shaker families living and working in as many as sixty buildings, only seven structures still survive in their entirety. These are owned by the Brothers of Christian Instruction, the religious order that purchased the Village and its more than 1,000 acres from the financially

Courtesy the United Society of Shakers, Sabbathday Lake

Elder Henry Green about to leave Alfred on a sales trip.

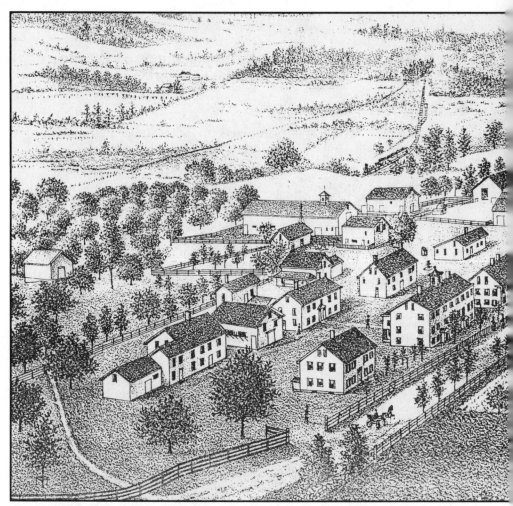

Courtesy the United Society of Shakers, Sabbathday Lake

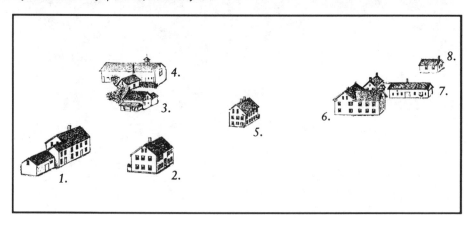

1.   2.   3.   4.   5.   6.   7.   8.

1880 view of Alfred, drawn by Phares F. Goist of Biddeford;
the buildings on the left side of the road are Church Family;
on the right, Second Family; and in the distance, North
Family. The illustration at left shows the buildings that
remain standing today.

1. Sisters' Shop/Laundry
2. Girls' Shop
3. Dairy
4. Cow Barn
5. Brethren's Shop
6. Trustees' Office
7. Office Carriage Shed
8. School House

pressed Believers. Over two centuries, a number of other buildings were lost to fires, interior woodwork was removed and sold to antique dealers, and, more recently, the Brothers completely renovated several buildings and razed others.

Of the seventeen buildings that once belonged to the North Family, only the ruins of the mill race remain. Those Church Family buildings still standing are inhabited by the Brothers, who have for decades remained on friendly terms with the Shakers, especially with those from Sabbathday Lake, Maine.

"Simple Gifts" from Alfred

It is said that "Simple Gifts," the most famous of Shaker songs, was composed at Alfred around 1848 by Elder Joseph Brackett. Elder Joseph is also claimed by the short-lived Society in Gorham (1784-1819), which he helped found when he first became a Shaker at the turn of the 19th century.

Planning Your Visit

There is no site interpretation in Alfred, but information about the former community is available from the Museum at the Shaker Village of Sabbathday Lake, about fifty miles to the north.

The site map indicates the remaining Shaker structures including the 1913 Dwelling House, which is the third house on the same foundation, the previous two destroyed by fire. In the 1960s the roof and ell of this building also were consumed in a fire, and a flat roof was constructed to replace the original.

The Girls' House, pre-Shaker in origin, was moved by the Believers over the ice and up "Shaker Hill" to this site in 1796. The interior has been completely changed, but it once housed young girls and work rooms for sisters. The Brethren's Shop, ca. 1820, was remodeled in the 1870s; it too has been completely changed.

The Sisters' Shop/Laundry, built in the 1820s, was also done over. The building that was used as the Dairy after 1870 (also remodeled) was previously a cobbler's shop called "The Red Shoe Shop." Other structures include the Trustees' Office, Cow Barn, and Cart and Carriage House.

Alfred's School House is no longer at the site, having been given to the American Legion, who moved it to Shaker Pond, a few hundred yards from the Village.

Access to Alfred

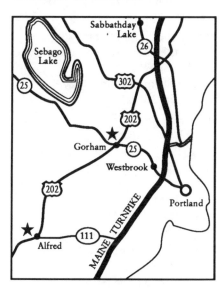

DIRECTIONS: The former Shaker community is on Route 202, just north of the town center of Alfred. It can be reached from Biddeford, which is about 10 miles to the east, by Route 111; if traveling from Sanford and points west, Alfred is 3 miles northeast on Route 202 (locally 4A); from the north, take 202 south.

The original Horse Stable was sold to neighbors who moved it across the ice of the nearby lake.

There is also a Shaker cemetery in Alfred, with a single granite marker in the middle. This cemetery still belongs to the order. The community's bell, used to call Believers to meals and worship, has been transferred to the Sabbathday

For further site/tour information contact:

Museum of Sabbathday Lake
The United Society of Shakers
RR 1, Box 640
Poland Spring, Maine 04274
Tel: 207/926-4597

Berkshire Shaker Seminars
1350 West Street
Pittsfield, Massachusetts 01201
(Tour information only)

For lodging/dining information contact:

The Maine Publicity Bureau
Yarmouth Information Center
P. O. Box 1057
Yarmouth, Maine 04096
Tel: 207/846-0833

*Canterbury Sisters at their
post office at the turn
of the century.*

CANTERBURY SHAKER VILLAGE

"Holy Ground"
Canterbury, New Hampshire
1792-1992

Shakers Lived There Until 1992

Museum, Exhibits, Tours

Special Programs

Gift Shop & Restaurant

A strikingly beautiful site, Canterbury sits on a hilltop, with a panoramic view of New Hampshire fields and woods. This was the sixth village founded by the Shakers.

Until 1992, when the last sister died, Canterbury was one of only two surviving communities with resident Shakers. For the last half of this century it was the center of Shaker affairs —the home of Shaker eldresses who administered Shakerdom. Today, Canterbury is managed by Canterbury Shaker Village, Inc., a nonprofit educational corporation.

Canterbury was one of the wealthier Shaker communities, as can be seen in the still-handsome remaining buildings —twenty-four of them, on 694 acres. Maintenance and restoration are done with an eye to authenticity. The time period evoked at Canterbury is approximately 1910 in spirit, including the way traditional crafts and handiwork are carried out by those who demonstrate in the workshops.

The Village has undertaken a careful restoration effort involving several of the buildings. Another project is restora-

Photo: Golden Hill Press

The 1792 Meetinghouse, right, is one of six still standing of the total eleven built by Moses Johnson; the 1848 Ministry Shop is at left.

tion of the apple orchard, which had become overgrown by 1990, when a local men's group volunteered to cut away the brush and weeds. The Canterbury Shakers had always taken great pride in their apples, and many old varieties of trees were rescued by this effort. Work has been underway to replant some of the missing varieties. The clearing of the old apple orchard also opened up a scenic view considered one of the prettiest in the state.

History of the Site

Founded in 1792, Canterbury celebrated its bicentennial in 1992. At its peak in the 1850s, there were 300 people here, in 100 buildings on 4,000 acres.

For decades, Canterbury was important as a regional headquarters, or bishopric. Always a spiritual and intellectual focus for the Shakers, Canterbury's leaders usually had close ties with the Central Ministry at New Lebanon. In 1960, after the closing of Hancock, the Village became the residence of the Central Ministry.

Leading Shakers have lived at Canterbury, and it was one of the most progressive Shaker communities in terms of its relationships with the outside world. Canterbury Shakers often differed from stricter Believers, being more flexible and open-minded when associating with the "world's people." They were active in social movements and public speaking, interested in subjects ranging from women's suffrage to pacifism.

Emerson and Hawthorne at Canterbury

In the late 19th century, Canterbury was the printing center for all Shakerdom. There were always important Shaker editors and writers here, producing periodicals and theological writings. Author and philosopher Ralph Waldo Emerson and his friend writer Nathaniel Hawthorne visited the Shakers more than once, Emerson having been at Canterbury during the late 1820s and Hawthorne going there in 1831. (Hawthorne also also spent time with the Shakers at Harvard, Massachusetts.)

Canterbury prospered thanks to its able leadership, profiting from agriculture, the seed industry, herbal medicines, textile production, and handiwork.

Eldress Emma B. King of Canterbury was a key Shaker leader during the mid-20th century. Elevated to the Central Ministry in 1946, Eldress Emma, until her death in 1966, made many of the decisions to dispose of the order's property, cooperating with collectors and museums that recognized the importance of preserving the Shaker heritage for posterity.

The last surviving member of the Shaker Central Ministry was Bertha Lindsay, who died at Canterbury in 1990. Sister Bertha was instrumental in establishing the first museum at Canterbury.

The nonprofit corporation, Canterbury Village, Inc., was established in 1969 to manage and care for the site. Its profes-

Young Shaker Sisters at Canterbury enjoy a moment together beside their modern truck in the early 1900s.

sional staff—with essential and extensive volunteer assistance—handles among other things the historical interpretation of Canterbury as well as public relations and guided tours, and administers the library and archives.

Canterbury Shaker Village, a cluster of 23 buildings atop a hill surrounded by fields and woodlots, makes you "kindly welcome."

Planning Your Visit

CANTERBURY
Shaker Village

From May through October guided tours are offered daily through five of the restored buildings. (During April and in November and December this tour covers three buildings and is supplemented by craft demonstrations and other programs, such as musical performances.) Guided tours last ninety minutes; the last starts at 4 p.m.

The guided tour includes stops at the 1792 Meetinghouse, the 1848 Ministry Shop, the 1817 Sisters' Shop, the 1795 Laundry, and the 1823 School House. These buildings are furnished with original Shaker artifacts, and the guides explain Shaker traditions and offer anecdotes to illustrate everyday life at the community.

Other buildings open to visitors include the restored 1806 Carpenter's Shop, where oval boxmaking, dovetailing and basket-weaving are carried out. Also, the 1819 Horse Barn is open, with an exhibit of

horse-drawn carriages and sleighs from the region, most of which are not Shaker. Other buildings at Canterbury, not included in the tour, are the 1793 Dwelling House, the 1797 Syrup Shop, the 1810 Childrens' House, the 1811 Infirmary, the 1820 Cart Shed, the 1824 Brethren's Shop, the 1825 Carriage House, the 1826 Enfield House, the 1830 Trustees' Office, the 1837 Bee House, the 1841 North Shop, the 1905 Creamery, the 1908 Fire House, the 1910 Power House, and the 1923 Garage, many of which are open to the public.

SPECIAL PROGRAMS

Canterbury holds a number of "special-event days" throughout the year, including Mother Ann Day in early August, Wool Day and Herb Day in May, an Antiques Show and Sale in late August, Wool Day in September, and Harvest Day in October. These and other special days are celebrated with demonstrations, speakers on Shaker life, exhibits, crafts, and other activities such as demonstrations of old-time agricultural methods.

There are a number of educational programs throughout the

Courtesy Canterbury Shaker Village

Retiring room occupied by Elder Henry C. Blinn (1824-1905), Ministry Shop.

The 1823 School House at Canterbury, restored in 1992, is included in the guided tour program.

regular months the village is open, including lectures, day-long craft workshops, and two-day craft workshops with overnight accommodation.

Herb and vegetable gardens, nature trails, and picnic tables are available to the public.

Shaker items such as brooms, oval boxes, poplarware, herbal commodities, baskets, and textiles are made on site and sold in the Gift Shop of the 1825 Carriage House. An exhibit of Shaker artifacts is in this building, which also houses demonstrations of crafts such as weaving, spinning, woodworking, and broom-making. The shop also has Shaker reproductions and books for sale.

Visitors can begin or end their tour with a "Shaker-inspired" lunch, offered daily at the Creamery Restaurant, and on Sundays a brunch is served. From May through October the restaurant offers a candlelight dinner on Fridays and Saturdays, combined with a tour of the Village. The Summer Kitchen in the 1910 Power House offers baked goods and light take-out foods prepared fresh daily.

Facilities are available for conferences, meetings, receptions, and as retreats.

Hours: Open May-October daily; Monday-Saturday 10 a.m.-5 p.m., Sunday noon-5 p.m.; April, November & December, open Friday & Saturday, 10 a.m.-5 p.m.; Sunday noon-5 p.m.

The Creamery Restaurant is open daily April through December for lunch, 11:30 a.m.-2:30 p.m., and Sundays for brunch 11 a.m.-2 p.m. Candlelight dinners on Fridays and Saturdays at 7 p.m. are offered year-round by reservation.

For further site/tour information contact:

Canterbury Shaker Village
288 Shaker Road
Canterbury, NH 03224
Tel: 603/783-9511

For lodging/dining information contact:

Concord Area Chamber of Commerce
Concord, NH 03301
Tel: 603/224-2508

Admission Fee

Limited Handicapped Access

Restrooms

No Pets

Major Credit Cards Accepted

Dining

Access to Canterbury

DIRECTIONS: Canterbury Shaker Village is in Canterbury, New Hampshire, 20 miles north of Concord and 20 minutes south of Laconia and the Lakes Region. From I-93 take Exit 18 and follow signs 6.7 miles to the Village. From Route 106, turn onto Shaker Road and travel north to the Village.

The "Festival of Shaker Crafts and
Herbs" is held the first Saturday of
June at Lower Shaker Village, Enfield,
New Hampshire.

ENFIELD

"Chosen Vale"
Enfield, New Hampshire
1793-1923

> *Museum & Exhibits*
> *Self-guided Walking Tour*
> *Herb & Vegetable Gardens, Special Events*
> *Gift Shop, Dining & Lodging*

The first Enfield Shaker was James Jewett, who in 1782 was converted after meeting Shaker missionaries while he was supervising the construction of a bridge in Enfield Village. Jewett offered his home as a meeting place for other Believers and would-be Believers.

Despite some local opposition from hostile neighbors, the little group at Enfield grew until it was able, in 1793, to purchase land in a pleasant valley beside Mascoma Lake, and the Enfield Shaker community was established. The Village eventually had three families, with more than 300 Believers.

The core of the present Enfield site consists of the eight buildings in a complex known as "Lower Shaker Village." The most impressive structure is the six-story Great Stone Dwelling, ca. 1841. When first built, this was the tallest building north of Boston. The Village considers the Dwelling to be its "landmark structure," and it is the least altered of all the original buildings on the site.

The Dwelling is operated by a private corporation as an inn and restaurant, and is called "The Shaker Inn." This part-

The Great Stone Dwelling at Enfield, New Hampshire was New England's largest stone building outside Boston when it was built in 1837-41.

nership also rents rooms to the public in other buildings on the site, including the Bethany House and the Ministry Shop.

History of the Site

Enfield turned out to be quite prosperous and is said to have been one of the initiators of the thriving seed-packaging industry for which the Shakers were famous all over the United States. Enfield Shakers were also known for their medicinal herb industry and are credited for inventing "Lucifer" book matches as well as a turbine water wheel.

In 1927 the Village was sold to a Catholic order, the Congregation of the Missionaries of Our Lady of La Salette. Of the dozens of buildings the Shakers erected in their more than 130 years at Enfield, only thirteen remain. (Eight more have been relocated within the area.) Five now belong to a private partnership that purchased the site from the Catholic

Enfield Shaker Village, ca. 1870.

order in 1985. A nonprofit corporation, The Museum at Lower Shaker Village, owns the Laundry/Dairy, Stone Mill Building, and West Meadows Barn. The Catholic order still owns five buildings from the North Family.

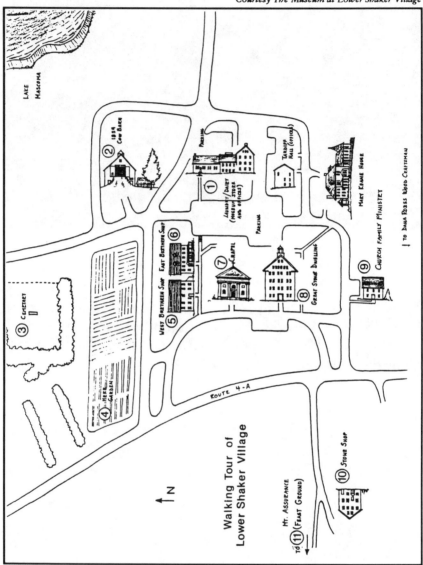

Site Map of Lower Shaker Village, Enfield.

Planning Your Visit

The "Shaker Revels" outdoor musical production is set against the village backdrop.

Among the thirteen Shaker buildings remaining at Enfield is the three-part Laundry/Dairy, which began as an 1813 dairy and has been added to over the centuries. In it are the Museum and the Shaker Store, the latter housed in an addition dated 1944.

These structures show the kinds of building methods and materials used by the Shakers. Their wood-paneled walls with beaded finishes and walls of built-in drawers and cupboards are classic examples of what the Believers made and used. Other buildings that can be viewed on a self-guided walking tour include the 1854 Cow Barn, said to have been one of the best of its day and the largest surviving Shaker barn, the 1820 West Brethren Shop and East Brethren Shop, the Great Stone Dwelling, 1880 Ministry Building, and 1849 Stone Mill Building.

Not every building at Enfield is Shaker. The 1930 Mary Keane Memorial Chapel on the grounds is used for weddings and organ recitals. This chapel was built by the La Salette Brothers. Mary Keane, a benefactress of the Brothers, also built a Victorian home nearby, which is now a private inn.

On the site also is the Shaker Cemetery (1793-1928), marked by a single granite stone and the resting place for 330 Believers. Mount Assurance, the Enfield Shaker Feast Ground, overlooks the Village and surrounding area.

Attractive Gardens

Consistent with the Shaker reputation as leading agriculturalists, the Village has developed an 11,000 sq. ft. herb garden which serves as a setting for educational programs. The herbs are gathered and processed as part of the living-history demonstrations by museum staff.

Visitors need at least an hour or two for the self-guided tour and to enjoy the sights and smells of the herb garden, watch skilled artisans demonstrating traditional Shaker crafts, and learn the story of the Enfield Shakers through exhibits of furniture, tools and clothing. The Shaker Store and Shaker Inn complete the visit.

Throughout the year there are crafts demonstrations and workshops. Special events at Enfield include a late spring "Festival of Shaker Crafts and Herbs"; a summer production of Shaker music and the written word; also in the summer, a Silent Auction of handcrafted articles and an annual Antique Show and Sale. A "Shaker Harvest Festival" in autumn features cider-pressing, children's entertainment, traditional music and dance, and sheepdog demonstrations.

At the holidays, there is a free "Holiday Gift Extravaganza," with handmade items for sale and also special pastries and hot beverages served throughout the day by The Shaker Inn. A "Christmas Cookie Fair" offers more than 100 varieties of homemade cookies, sold by the pound.

Tourist Information

Museum and Store Hours: June 1-October 15, Monday through Saturday 10 a.m.-5 p.m., Sunday noon-5 p.m.; October 16-May 31, Saturday 10 a.m.-4 p.m., Sunday noon-4 p.m.

The Shaker Inn: Open year-round; breakfast served daily; (winter hours) November 1-May 31, 8-11 a.m.; (summer hours) June 1-October 31, begins at 7:30 a.m.; lunch served daily during summer, 11:30 a.m.-2 p.m.; in winter, Saturday and Sunday only; dinner served Wednesday-Sunday in winter, also Tuesday in summer. The Inn has a variety of accommodations available, with private baths and furnished with Shaker reproductions.

For further site/tour information contact:

Lower Shaker Village
2 LSV
Enfield, New Hampshire 03748
Tel: 603/632-4346

The Shaker Inn
11 LSV
Enfield, New Hampshire 03748
Tel: 603/632-7800

For additional lodging/dining information contact:

New Hampshire Office of Travel & Tourism Development
Box 856
Concord, New Hampshire 03302-0856
Tel: 603/271-2343

 Admission Fee

 Limited Handicapped Access

 Restrooms

 No Pets

 Major Credit Cards Accepted

 Dining

 Lodging

Access to Enfield

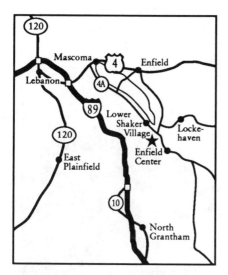

DIRECTIONS: Lower Shaker Village is on Route 4A in Enfield, 12 miles southeast of Hanover, in eastern New Hampshire. Take Exit 17 off I-89, then Route 4 east to 4A south; follow signs.

Illustration of Tyringham,
mid-19th century.

TYRINGHAM

"City of Love"
Tyringham, Massachusetts
1792-1875

Self-Guided & Guided Tours

Among the earliest of Shaker villages, Tyringham was also one of the smallest. Today a dozen of its buildings remain, all privately owned.

Rising on a slope in the steep Berkshire Mountains of Massachusetts, Tyringham was fairly isolated and suffered harsh winters and a short growing season.

Its closure in 1875, after eighty-three often difficult years, marked the beginning of a period for the Shakers that historian Stephen J. Stein called "the Transformation of the Society" and a "time of creative adjustment to rapidly changing circumstances."

As the United States marked its centennial, the order had passed through the age of the founders, then the middle period that was at first revivalist, and later a consolidating period slashed by the Civil War. By 1875, Shakers were more of the world than ever before, their burgeoning industries famous for their quality. Now, however, there also were fundamental problems: lack of new permanent members, compounded by the aging and loss of long-time members.

Tyringham also experienced internal dissension, which caused a large group to leave in 1858, and another one in the early 1870s. The closing of Tyringham with its fewer than twenty surviving Believers, was the beginning of a series of retrenchments that continued until 1960, when Hancock itself shut down.

History of the Site

Several Tyringham residents first became interested in Ann Lee's teachings as early as 1782 and began meeting in their own homes. As often happened to the early Shakers, they met hostility from neighbors. They persevered, sometimes being supported by visits from major Shaker leaders such as Father William Lee and James Whittaker. The group was first "gathered" as a society in 1792, the same year as Canterbury, New Hampshire and Enfield, Connecticut.

Three families lived here, in a setting described in Shakerism as a "remarkable place...being built against the side of the mountain." Some houses were two stories on the side facing the road and four stories in the rear. More than 3,000 acres were in the hands of the society, including tillage land a few hundred feet below the level of the community. A complex system of drainage and stone waterworks still covers the mountainside above and below the sites of the three families.

As it was with other Shaker communities, the industrious Tyringham Brethren in their old-fashioned broad-brimmed hats were to be found out on the road, selling garden seed in their one-horse wagons. The seed business at Tyringham was fairly large-scale, as was broom-making and the manufacture of ox yokes and ax helves. Tiny and remote as it was, Tyringham did make its mark in the world, being especially known for the manufacture of excellent rakes.

A few miles to the northwest in West Stockbridge the society acquired and then ran a forge mill, which still stands at the bridge in the center of town.

At Tyringham, no buildings remain from the South Family. Church and North buildings were used as resorts for

Early in the 20th century, vacationers enjoyed strolling near the Tyringham Shaker Mill on the Nokomis Lodge Estate.

Tyringham Shaker Mill on the Nokomis Lodge Estate.

a time, when the Berkshires were discovered in the late 19th century as an attractive haven for tourists and seekers after health cures. The Church Family site was operated as "Fernside" by Dr. Joseph Jones, who swapped land in Pennsylvania with the Shakers to complete its sale. The North Family Dairy became "Nokomis Lodge."

Modifications and demolitions of Shaker buildings at Tyringham continued throughout the years. In 1925, the Meetinghouse was moved a mile away to the Leavenworth Farm, eventually to be acquired by playwright Sidney Howard. The mammoth five-and-a-half-story Church family

Seed House was partly dismantled four years later, the upper portion being rebuilt two miles down and across the valley.

Courtesy Robert Meader

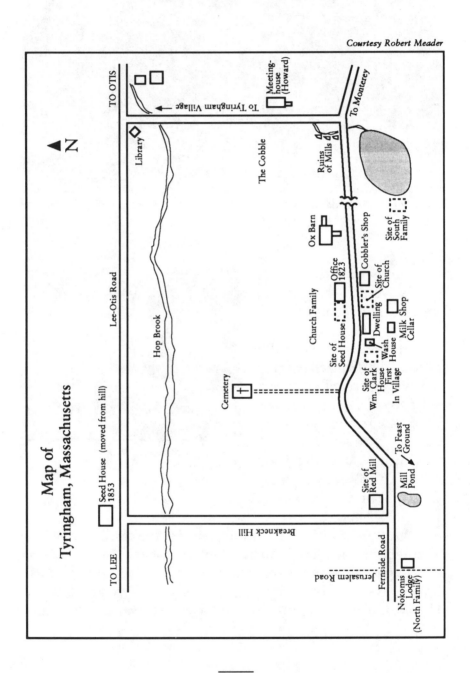

Map of
Tyringham, Massachusetts

Planning Your Visit

Among the structures remaining, all of which are privately owned, are the bottom level of the huge Seed House, which has its datestone under the eave, an unusual feature; the 1792 Meetinghouse, which has been attached to a farmhouse; the Church Family 1823 Trustees' Office; the Ox Barn; and the Wagon Shed. Please respect the owners' privacy.

The cemetery where ninety-nine Believers are buried is also accessible.

Also at Tyringham are the Cobbler's Shop; an unusual mounting block at the former site of the removed Meetinghouse; the Church family Dwelling with bell cupola and behind it a Shop building. There is a Cheese House with a roof of a single stone slab; the Red Mill, North family Dairy, and a small Shaker Shed also still stand in view, and ruins and foundation stones of other buildings can be seen.

Access to Tyringham

DIRECTIONS: Tyringham is between Monterey to the south and Lee to the north. It can be reached from Exit 2 of the Massachusetts Pike (I-90), and sits squarely on the Appalachian Trail.

Tourist Information

Tours and study groups of the Tyringham site are offered by Hancock Shaker Village, or visitors can do a self-guided tour from the road.

For further site/tour information contact:

Hancock Shaker Village
PO Box 898
Pittsfield, Massachusetts 01202
Tel: 413/443-0188

For lodging/dining information contact:

Berkshire Visitors Bureau
Berkshire Common
West Street
Pittsfield, Massachusetts 01202
Tel: 413/443-9186

The Marble Shaft at Harvard, commemorating the beating of James Whittaker and William Lee by a mob. From Gleanings from Old Shaker Journals.

HARVARD AND FRUITLANDS

"Lovely Vineyard"
Harvard, Massachusetts
1791-1918

>*Square House*
>
>*Museums, Library, Exhibits*
>
>*Self-Guided Tour & Special Programs*
>
>*Museum Shop & Tea Room*

Listed on the National Register of Historic Places, Harvard is one of the most important Shaker sites. It was here in the Square House, the home of a New Light Baptist preacher, that Mother Ann Lee made her first converts during her 1781-1783 missionary journey.

In this house, in 1782, Mother Ann was threatened by a local mob incensed by the conversion of family members to the Shaker faith. The mob included some militiamen fresh from the bloodshed of the Revolution, who despised the Shaker leaders because they were English. They ultimately drove the Shaker men, including James Whittaker and William Lee, out of town, cruelly lashing them and striking them with sticks for miles down the road. Whittaker and Meacham suffered a particularly severe beating near the future site of the South Family Office, where the Shakers later erected a marble monument, the Whipping Stone.

For all the early tribulations at Harvard, the Shakers stayed and settled here, considering the site to have been

Harvard at the turn of the century; Meetinghouse is on right. From Shakerism.

consecrated, as it were, by the suffering and Mother Ann's persecution.

More than a dozen buildings still remain of the original thirty, along with foundations, a cemetery, and an outdoor worship place constructed in 1842. The houses are all in private hands, but a self-guided walking tour (or drive) can be taken.

Harvard is very near to and should be seen in conjunction with Fruitlands, the first Shaker museum in the United States when it opened in 1922. The Harvard Historical Society also has some material from the Harvard (and Shirley) Shakers.

History of the Site

In 1791, Harvard was the fourth Shaker community to be "called into Gospel order." In time it became one of the most scrutinized by influential individuals from "the world," because it was the closest Shaker society to a major metropolitan area (Boston).

Harvard's Believers had regular contact and exchanges of ideas with distinguished New Englanders such as Nathaniel Hawthorne, Bronson Alcott, and Ralph Waldo Emerson. In the mid-19th century, Alcott created Fruitlands, a Utopian community in Harvard, which brought him into regular contact with the Shakers. When it failed, in 1844, some of its members joined the Shaker community. The now-restored Fruitlands farmhouse, which was owned by Bronson Alcott, is at the Fruitlands Museums.

Harvard was quite prosperous, with many industries. The Shakers had cattle, sheep, poultry and sold butter and cheese. Their herb industry provided medicine and herbs throughout the area. Their mill turned out spools, broom handles, furniture, and wooden sieves. They grew corn, oats, rye, buckwheat and vegetables, and sold fruit and fruit trees. Their South Family Stone Barn was built from "turkey feather" fan money. They dyed cloth made by the Sisters, and invented a chimney cap, also widely sold. They were also book binders. Other products were apple sauce, elderberry and currant wines, and pumpkins.

The "Holy Hill of Zion" was the name given to a hilltop west of the Village in 1842, during a period of revival in which all the Shaker communities were directed to establish an outdoor place of worship. The families at Harvard cleared and leveled it over a two-year period, erecting an inscribed "Fountain Stone" in a central plot and installing outdoor seating.

Shakers would sing as they marched together up the hill for their services in this private place of worship. Forming a double circle around the Fountain Stone, they listened to addresses. Part of the ceremony was the "consuming" of a "spiritual meal" offered by entities of the spirit world with whom they claimed to have contact. The Believers received "gifts" from the spirit world through those members who were considered "instruments," and they sang, testified, and marched for hours.

When these outdoor meeting sites eventually came into disuse, each community hid or destroyed its Fountain Stone. The only one ever recovered whole was the stone from Groveland, New York.

At its peak, there were about 200 persons living in the four families of the Harvard community: Church, now known as "Shaker Village," with nine buildings still standing; North, with only one remaining house, which is on Shaker Road at the Harvard-Ayer town line; South, which has several buildings left, on South Shaker Road; and East Family, whose buildings were dismantled when Route 2 was constructed.

Sold by the Shakers in 1899, the South Family buildings were variously used as a home-canning club, a summer camp for city children and, in the case of the Dwelling House, as a chicken coop. In the early 1960s, the Boston Museum of Fine Arts installed in its Shaker Gallery an exhibit of interior woodwork taken from this building. The furniture collection in the gallery is gone, and the gallery closed, but the woodwork is still at the museum.

Harvard and nearby Shirley, part of which is now a state prison, were part of the same Shaker bishopric.

Fruitlands

Fruitlands on Prospect Hill Road, a few minutes' drive from the former Harvard Shaker community, is itself designated a state and national historic landmark. Fruitlands has beautiful grounds and four distinct museums, including one housed in a relocated Shaker building. (This is the Trustees' Office, originally built at Harvard's Church Family in 1794.) The other museums are Fruitlands Farmhouse, once a retreat for the Transcendentalists; Picture Gallery, a first-rate collection of American paintings; and American Indian Museum, with relics, dioramas, and statues.

The Fruitlands Museums were founded in 1914 by Clara Endicott Sears, philanthropist, writer, and prominent Boston-

The Shaker Museum at Fruitlands.

ian, on property she used as a summer home. A close friend of the Shakers, Miss Sears acquired the original Shaker Trustees' Office from Harvard in 1918, after the community had closed. Miss Sears wanted the Trustees' Office to accompany the 18th-century (non-Shaker) farmhouse she was preserving on the property.

Moving the Shaker Office to her 200 acres of land at a site close to Bronson Alcott's Fruitlands, she insisted on authentic restoration and took even the original foundation, fence, and stone steps trod by Mother Ann, along with the Office building.

The museum is filled with artifacts forming an early example of the collecting of first-quality objects of Shaker workmanship. There is also a fine collection of journals, music books and manuscripts in the museum library. The museum continues to collect material relating to the Harvard and Shirley communities.

The South Family Dwelling, Harvard, as it appears today.

Clara Endicott Sears was one of the first to publish a book of collected original Shaker writings: *Gleanings from Old Shaker Journals* tells the story of Mother Ann's missionary work and journey; it also relates how the Harvard Shakers lived and worshiped. First published in 1916, it spoke of the last Harvard Believers with affection and respect. With the Shaker Museum at Fruitlands, Clara Endicott Sears took a leading part in the preservation of the Shaker heritage. Thanks to her work, Fruitlands and Harvard Shaker Village are now inseparably linked (though unofficially) for those who visit the two sites.

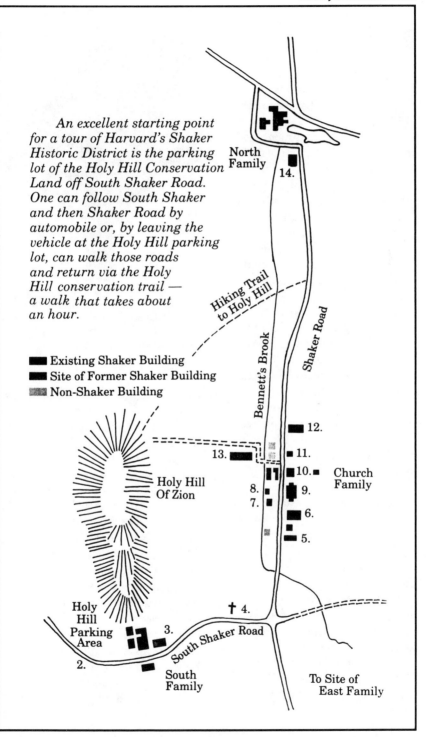

An excellent starting point for a tour of Harvard's Shaker Historic District is the parking lot of the Holy Hill Conservation Land off South Shaker Road. One can follow South Shaker and then Shaker Road by automobile or, by leaving the vehicle at the Holy Hill parking lot, can walk those roads and return via the Holy Hill conservation trail — a walk that takes about an hour.

North Family

Hiking Trail to Holy Hill

Bennett's Brook

Shaker Road

■ Existing Shaker Building
■ Site of Former Shaker Building
▨ Non-Shaker Building

14.

12.
13. ■ ■ 11.
■ 10. ■ Church Family
8. ■ ■ 9.
7. ■
■ 6.
■ 5.

Holy Hill Of Zion

Holy Hill Parking Area

2.
3.

† 4.

South Shaker Road

South Family

To Site of East Family

Courtesy Fruitlands Museums

Planning Your Visit

Educational and cultural programming and demonstrations are held year-round at Fruitlands and the site is open weekdays. Guided tours are offered by appointment, and a self-guided walking tour is available. A gift shop has Shaker reproductions—boxes, baskets, furnishings—books, and children's items.

A brochure prepared by the "Shaker 200 Committee" to celebrate Harvard's 200th Anniversary in 1991 is available at the Public Library and at Fruitlands. It suggests beginning the tour at the parking lot of the Holy Hill Conservation Land off South Shaker Road. If driving, follow South Shaker Road and then turn left onto Shaker Road; if walking, leave the car at the parking lot, follow those roads, and return via the Holy Hill Conservation Trail.

From Holy Hill, go left on South Shaker Road, past the remaining buildings of South Family. (These are all privately owned; respect the owners' privacy.) These are the ca. 1800 Family Shop, used commercially by the Shakers to make applesauce, and the 1830 South Family Dwelling House, both on the left side of the road. Just beyond are the ruins of the 1835 Stone Barn. Part of the foundations of the family's Office Building can be seen across the road.

Next on the left is the Shaker Cemetery, established in 1792 and distinctive for its "lollipop"

In 1879, Harvard substituted cast-iron grave markers for individual stone ones and is the only Shaker cemetery that retains them today.

cast-iron grave markers. The Cemetery, deeded to the Town of Harvard, contains the remains of more than 330 Shakers.

From the Cemetery, turn left onto Shaker Road. The first building on the right is thought to have been the Carpenter's Shop, and it is pre-1830. The second building on the right is the 1841 New Office, which has forty rooms and once housed trustees, hired help, and visitors. Fancy work produced by Sisters was sold in a shop on the first floor.

The next five structures on the right are all Shaker: the Meetinghouse, built in 1791, enlarged in 1857; the Ministry Shop, 1847, with carriage barn in the rear; the

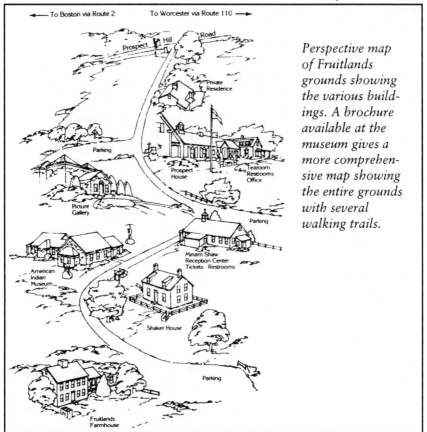

Perspective map of Fruitlands grounds showing the various buildings. A brochure available at the museum gives a more comprehensive map showing the entire grounds with several walking trails.

ca. 1800 Tailor's Shop; and the Square House, pre-1769, the best-known building on the site.

Across from the Meetinghouse, on the left side of Shaker Road, is the Second House, a 1795 dwelling; behind it is the Dry House, ca. 1845, a small stone structure used for drying herbs and fruits. Continuing through the Shaker Village to the end of Shaker Road, the North Family Office stands on a sharp, left-hand corner, the only remaining struc-

ture from that family's grouping, which once stood here. The family's mill ponds can still be seen across the road at the right and a grassy field bordered by tall maples along the roadside is the site of the large brick Dwelling House.

SPECIAL PROGRAMS: Call or write Fruitlands to find out about workshops and various activities, which include musical performances and year-round programming.

Harvard Historical Society has a collection of Shaker artifacts from both Harvard and Shirley, including journals, clothing, kitchenware, small furniture, photographs and letters. It is housed in the **Still River Baptist Meetinghouse,** a short distance from Fruitlands and Harvard.

Tourist Information

Guided tours of Harvard are sometimes available from Berkshire Shaker Seminars or the Boston Shaker Study Group.

Hours: Fruitlands Museums are open mid-May through late October, Tuesday through Sunday and Monday holidays; hours are 10 a.m.-5 p.m.

Refreshments and lunch are available in Prospect House when Fruitlands is open to the public. Picnic areas and nature trails are available for use by members and ticket holders.

The Museum Research Library is open year-round by appointment and houses primary source materials received by Miss Sears directly from the Harvard Shakers. The Museum Shop is open during normal hours and again from Thanksgiving to Christmas.

Harvard Historical Society is open Tuesdays 9 a.m.-5 p.m., and by appointment.

For further site/tour information contact:

Fruitlands Museums
102 Prospect Hill Road
Harvard, Massachusetts 01451
Tel: 508/456-3924

**Harvard Historical Society
Baptist Meetinghouse**
Still River Road (Route 110)
Still River, Massachusetts 01467
Tel: 508/456-8285

For additional lodging/dining information contact:

Worcester County Convention and Visitors Bureau
33 Waldo Street
Worcester, Massachusetts 01608
Tel: 508/753-2920
Fax. 508/754-8560

Admission Fee   Limited Handicapped Access   Restrooms   Leashed Pets Only

Major Credit Cards Accepted   Dining

Access to Harvard

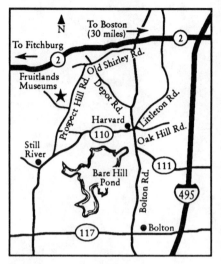

DIRECTIONS: Harvard, Massachusetts, is 3 miles west of I-495 and just south of Route 2, about 30 miles west of Boston.

Local Directions from Harvard, Massachusetts: To Fruitlands, head west on Route 110 and follow signs to the Museum, on Prospect Hill Road, about 2 miles away. To Harvard Shaker Village, head north from Harvard on Route 111, about 2 miles, and turn right on South Shaker Road.

From Boston and east: Take Route 2 west to the second Route 111 exit for Harvard; then take the first right onto Old Shirley Road. Museum will be on your right. Or take I-90 west to I-495 north to Route 111 exit. Follow local directions above.

From New York and south: Take I-95 north to I-495 north, then to Exit 28; head west on Route 111. Or take I-95 to I-91 in New Haven, Connecticut, and head north to I-90, the Massachusetts Pike; head east to I-495. Follow the local directions.

From the west: Take I-90 east to I-495 north; exit at Route 111. Follow the local directions.

From the north: Take I-495 south; exit at Route 2 West. Follow directions for Boston and east.

For the Harvard Historical Society: Take same exit (Route 111); take same right onto Old Shirley Road; follow Old Shirley Road to its end (about 2.5 miles) to Route 110 (Still River Road). Go about one mile to the Baptist Meetinghouse on the left side.

The Elijah Wilds house in Shirley, where Mother
Ann and the early Shakers were attacked by a mob.
From Gleanings from Old Shaker Journals,
compiled by Clara Endicott Sears.

SHIRLEY

"Pleasant Garden"
Shirley, Massachusetts
1793-1908

Site Where Mother Ann Faced Mob

First gathered in 1792, Shirley was founded the next year, the same time as communities at Alfred, Maine, and Enfield, New Hampshire, during an era of rapid growth for the Shakers. Shirley was the site of the 1783 persecution of Mother Ann and her followers during her missionary journey.

This Shaker site is currently part of the Massachusetts Correctional Institution (MCI) system. In the 1993 bicentennial year of the Shaker Village, considerable cooperation between the Shirley Historical Society and the MCI opened up several of the twelve remaining Shaker structures for tours under the supervision of MCI staff.

History of the Site
During Mother Ann's missionary journey in 1783, she stayed at the home of convert Elijah Wilds, which was surrounded by an angry mob opposed to the Shakers' proselytizing. After a long night of harassment, Mother Ann and the family offered food to the mob.

Ann's brother, William Lee, and James Whittaker agreed to leave and were escorted by the mob back to Harvard. It was there that the pair suffered a brutal beating. Father James was tied to a tree and whipped, and Father William was whipped while on his knees.

Shirley at the turn of the century.

In spite of these persecutions, the Shaker work went on. A strong group developed at Shirley, around the homes of Elijah and Ivory Wilds, who gave tracts of land to the order for its Village.

The Shirley Shakers prospered at first. In 1848 they built a large mill in the town of Shirley at great expense. The business did not succeed because of insufficient hands to run it properly, a problem which was to plague Shirley throughout its existence. The mill still exists, most recently operating as Samson Cordage Works.

Through much of the rest of the century Shirley was in economic difficulty and raised some funds by selling parcels of land. The three remaining Sisters joined the Harvard community in 1908, when the Central Ministry sold the remaining 889 acres, with twenty-six buildings, to the State of Massachusetts. Adapted at first as a school for troubled boys, the site was later incorporated into the Commonwealth's prison system.

Photo: Golden Hill Press

The former Shaker community at Shirley is now incorporated into a state correctional institution.

Courtesy Hancock Shaker Village

The Shirley 1793 Meetinghouse now stands in Hancock Shaker Village, where it was moved in 1962 to replace an identical building dismantled by the Shakers years earlier. The architect was Moses Johnson.

Courtesy Shirley Historical Society

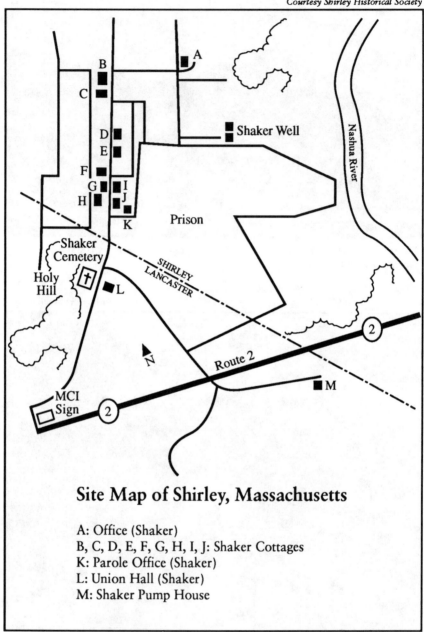

Site Map of Shirley, Massachusetts

A: Office (Shaker)
B, C, D, E, F, G, H, I, J: Shaker Cottages
K: Parole Office (Shaker)
L: Union Hall (Shaker)
M: Shaker Pump House

Planning Your Visit

Courtesy Hancock Shaker Village

The site map indicates the location of the twelve buildings within the prison that are thought to be Shaker. Among the buildings are the Church Family Ministry Shop, Office, Dwelling, Boys' House, and Wash House. Several other structures have been relocated. The frame Meetinghouse was moved to Hancock in 1962. The North Family structures are the Dwelling, which has been added to, and a large Shop, also referred to as an Office building. The Shaker Cemetery still remains, as does "Holy Hill," the site of outdoor worship services in the mid-19th century.

Two Shaker-used structures exist outside the prison, located south of the Shirley Road overpass on Route 2. One, the Brick Tavern, was purchased by the Shakers to lodge their guests. Opposite is a small, gambrel-roofed building moved from the Church Family to be used as an Infirmary. Both are privately owned and the owner's privacy should be respected.

Tours of Shaker sites and buildings in the prison complex are only by special arrangement with the prison administration through the Shirley Historical Society.

Fruitlands Museums
(See Harvard Chapter)

Believers at Shirley had close connections with their brethren and sisters in nearby Harvard, Massachusetts. As with Harvard, some of Shirley's history can be learned during a visit to Fruitlands which has what is considered the best collection of Shirley artifacts, which are scarce. These include a few pieces of furniture, textiles, sieves, labels, and a good selection of photographs and manuscripts.

Shirley Historical Society Museum

Located on Center Road in historic Shirley Center, about three miles north of the former Shaker site, the Museum has offered demonstrations of Shaker crafts, performances of Shaker music, dramatic readings, and lectures. The highlight of Shirley's 1993 bicentennial celebration was "The Flame Is Never Ceasing," a day-long program in conjunction with the Sabbathday Lake Shakers in October. Co-hosted by the Boston Area Shaker Study Group, this program included the Sabbathday Believers leading the singing of Shaker songs and answering questions about Shaker lifestyle, history, and beliefs.

The Society Museum has a Shaker room with exhibits and artifacts.

Tourist Information

Hours: Fruitlands Museums are open 10 a.m.-5 p.m. mid-May through late October, Tuesday through Sunday; closed Mondays. The Shirley Historical Society Museum is open Saturday, 10 a.m.-1 p.m. and by appointment.

Site interpretation is available from Fruitlands and the Shirley Historical Society. From time to time group tours are offered of the site by Shirley Historical Society.

For further site/tour information contact:

Shirley Historical Society
182 Center Road
P.O. Box 217
Shirley, Massachusetts 01464
Tel: 508/425-9328

Fruitlands Museums
102 Prospect Hill Road
Harvard, Massachusetts 01451
Tel: 508/456-3924

Access to Shirley

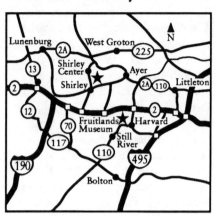

DIRECTIONS: Shirley is in north-central Massachusetts, near Harvard, another Shaker site. From Route 2, take the Shirley exit, and follow the signs for MCI. Public access to the site is restricted. To reach the Shirley Historical Society Museum follow Shirley Road north for 2 miles to Shirley. Then continue another 2 miles north on Center Road. The museum is on the left.

Admission Fee   Limited Handicapped Access   Restrooms   No Pets

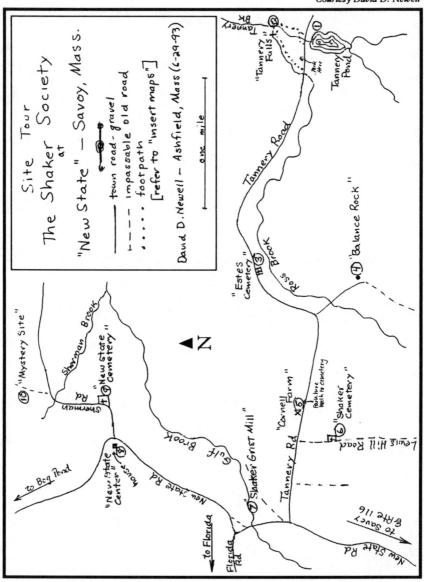

*Present-day site tour of Savoy,
drawn by David D. Newell.*

SAVOY

Savoy, Massachusetts
1817-1821

Only Foundations and Cellar Holes Remain
Self-guided & Guided Tours

This all but forgotten Shaker site in the northern Berkshire Mountains did not last long, but since there were as many as eighty Shakers living here in the early part of the 19th century it is considered one of the more noteworthy "out-families."

The remains of the Village—some foundations, cellar holes, and other stone remnants—lie in a wooded area mostly within Savoy State Forest. There are several remarkable natural wonders nearby which the Shakers visited, including the Balanced Rock and Tannery Falls. No contemporary sketches or photographs of Savoy have been found.

History of the Site

The only Shaker-authored commentary in print about Savoy is apocryphal. It recounts that one winter day, at the Second Family Office in Mount Lebanon, the Sisters in charge received a call from a woman of somewhat peculiar appearance who asked for something to eat.

Legend has it that it was because of this strange apparition that Savoy got its start. According to the book *Shakerism:* "An occurrence of curious psychic interest is narrated by those who have often heard it told by the participants.

"Food was given her, and while she ate she told of a wonderful revival that had been going on for some time in

Savoy, Massachusetts, a small town situated on a spur of the Green Mountain range.

"She said the people needed help. Throughout the interview she seemed careful that her face should not be seen and the sisters did not obtain a good look at her features. Rising at last and passing out, they watched her from the door; she walked unsteadily and, suddenly, while they were looking at her, vanished from sight. They decided they had been feeding and conversing with a spirit."

They also decided to look in on the revival at Savoy, where, tradition has it, the preaching of an "unrecognized" Baptist minister named Joseph Smith had stirred up the people of Savoy into a revivalist frenzy around 1810. After his departure (apparently after his wife appeared and objected to a second wife he had just taken), this religious stirring continued as a "New Light" revival. Although it had cooled slightly by 1816, the Shaker missionaries who travelled through the mountains to Savoy about 1819 found ready followers there. Soon there was a solid, though not formally "gathered" group of Believers. Eventually there were about eighty Shakers in the community.

Central to the Shaker community was the house of Shaker James Cornell. They attached their Meetinghouse (formerly a ballroom, in which they did their Shaker dancing) to Cornell's house. Across the road they built a three-story building which housed on the first floor a dairy, on the second a schoolroom, on the third rooms for visiting elders and teachers. Just east of the Meetinghouse they built a series of barns, and in 1818-1819 they also built a grist mill. Proctor Sampson, a well-to-do Shaker from Mount Lebanon, purchased other homes, buildings, and about 400 acres of land for the community, which eventually included about 1,500 mostly contiguous acres.

By 1820, the Shaker society at Savoy was a mix of traditional worldly practices and Shaker communitarianism. Most families continued to live in nuclear family arrangements and owned their homes and farms. Yet they were managing certain

Courtesy David D. Newell

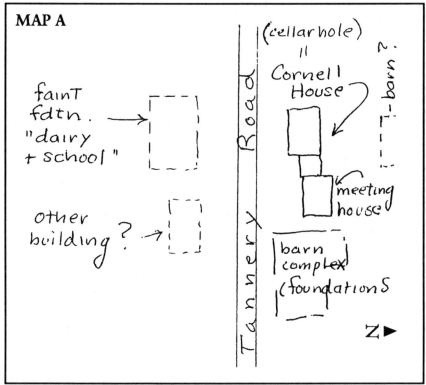

Present-day site tour of Savoy, drawn by David D. Newell.

other matters collectively. They associated in 1819 to construct a grist mill and purchased the land and built the mill "jointly." Many younger, and poorer, Believers lived together in a semi-communal state. Considerable lands and some buildings were owned by the Society and were improved and utilized collectively. The school was constructed and staffed and operated by the Society and without tax support.

The community began to prosper but was hit by drought two years running in 1820 and 1821. A plague of locusts also appeared in 1820 and by 1821 had become overwhelming. The Village had no forage or hay and became heavily dependent upon nearby Shaker communities.

At about this time, a new Shaker ministry, altered by the death in 1821 of Eldress Lucy Wright, sent a new emissary to

Courtesy David D. Newell

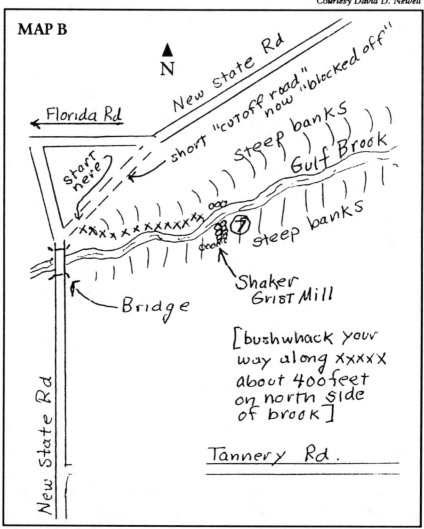

MAP B

N

Florida Rd

New State Rd

short "cutoff road" now "blocked off"

steep banks

Gulf Brook

start here

xxxx x x xxxxxxx

steep banks

Bridge

Shaker Grist Mill

[bushwhack your way along xxxxx about 400 feet on north side of brook]

New State Rd

Tannery Rd.

Present-day site tour of Savoy, drawn by David D. Newell.

Savoy. This midwesterner, used to the flat and deep Ohio soil, saw no promise in Savoy's hilly, rocky farms. The decision was made to disperse the Savoy Shakers to other villages, and between September and December of 1821 they were resettled at societies New Lebanon and Watervliet, New York. Some,

Courtesy David D. Newell

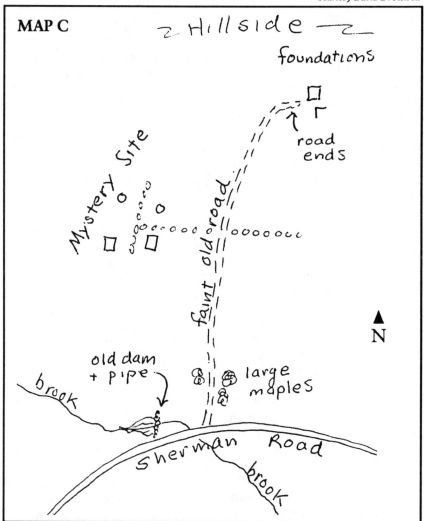

Present-day site tour of Savoy, drawn by David D. Newell.

homesick for Savoy, returned here and are buried in the local cemeteries. Shakers continued to use the land into the 1850s for summer pasture and herb gathering, and they leased out the grist mill. It was not until the late 1880s that all the land passed from Shaker ownership.

Planning Your Visit

Remaining foundations, cellar holes, and other stone remnants give the visitor a sense of the layout of the community. These include the James Cornell House, the Meetinghouse, the Dairy and the Grist Mill. There are also several cemeteries and other historical ruins, as well as places of great natural beauty which were known to the Shakers.

Guided tours are available through local historian David Newell, who has studied this site for several decades and has supplied much material, and the maps, for this chapter. The maps can be used for a self-guided tour, or guided tours are available. Most sites can be reached by conventional car, although four-wheel drive is recommended. Sturdy hiking shoes also, as some sites require a short walk through brush. Look out for bears!

Tannery Pond is so-called because in the mid-1800s (long after the Shakers had left) a small village existed here centered around a leather-tanning industry. Several house foundations can still be seen along the road.

Tannery Falls is one of the highest waterfalls in Massachusetts. New Lebanon Shakers came here in 1821, searching for high-elevation, wild medicinal herbs. Estes Cemetery is on the left (going west) side of Tannery Road, almost obscured by spruces. Savoy has many such small, early-1800s graveyards. The Estes family "split" during the religious revivals of the 1810s, with Thomas, his wife Betsy, and his brother Daniel joining the Shakers. Daniel later fell away from the faith and remained in Savoy until he died.

Balance Rock is a massive glacial boulder, a remnant of the Ice Age, left precariously balanced on a ledge. This is one-time Shaker land, and Shaker John Sherman and family lived nearby.

As you go west and bear westerly along Tannery Road (less than a mile from the parking place for Tannery Falls) you will see some old maples on both sides of the road at the top of a slight hill. The old cellar hole (filled with weeds) on your right is the Cornell House. There are other foundations (see Map A). Here was the center and heart of the Shaker Society at Savoy.

Lewis Hill road is rough and heavily washed out. Proceed by foot until you see a lovely cemetery surrounded by a fine stone wall. The Shaker Cemetery—also known as Dunham—has about fifteen graves (six with tombstones). All are Shakers who died in the faith or apostatized. James Cornell is buried here. This cemetery was established by the Shakers about 1818.

The Shaker Grist Mill is a short walk down Gulph Brook (see Map B). Only parts of the foundation of the dam and the mill building survive. In 1818, Calvin Green proposed to the Savoy Shakers that they construct a grist mill. This was one of the first communal ventures of the Savoy Believers and proved successful. These ruins are virtually the only surviving relics of Shaker manufacture that remain here.

At New State Center are one of two remaining New State (not Shaker) buildings and the sites of the Church and School. The extant building is next to the site of Nathan Haskins, Jr., a noted Shaker. This was once the heart of a village.

New State Cemetery is a large and lovely rural cemetery, still maintained, deep in the woods. Several Shakers who later left New Lebanon and returned to Savoy are buried there, together with others who played a part in the Savoy story. Former Shaker Bernard Mill and wife Ursala, whose graves are marked, are among those who returned from New Lebanon.

It is a short walk from Sherman Road to a series of unexplained foundations on one-time Shaker land. These are on part of the lands purchased by Proctor Sampson (see Map C). There is some extraordinary stone work and evidence of considerable building activity. It can be speculated that this was the beginning of a "center" of development for young Believers, some too poor to own a house, or who were living in log cabins. More research is needed, however.

For further site/tour information contact:

David D. Newell
39 Steady Lane
Ashfield, Massachusetts 01330
Tel: 413/628-3240

Hancock Shaker Village
PO Box 898
Pittsfield, MA 01202
Tel: (413) 443-0188

For lodging/dining information contact:

Berkshire Visitors Bureau
Berkshire Common
West Street
Pittsfield, Massachusetts 01201
Tel: (413) 443-9186

Access to Savoy

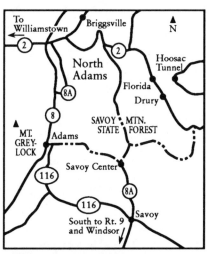

DIRECTIONS: Savoy State Forest is located roughly between Routes 2 and 116 running east and west near Savoy, Massachusetts. From

Pittsfield: Route 9 east to Windsor;
Route 8 north to Savoy. From
Adams: Route 116 east to Savoy.
From Northampton: Route 9 west
to Windsor; Route 8A north to
Savoy. To get to the Shaker
area take Center Road North from
Savoy (it intersects Route 116 near
Fire House just west of Savoy
Church); proceed about 3 miles on
Center Road to "T" with Adams
Road. Take a left; travel Adams
Road west several hundred feet to
first right, turn onto New State
Road (New State Road is "semi-
paved" and rough—go slow);
continue north on New State Road
about 1.5 miles to Tannery Road.
Take a right turn onto Tannery
Road. If you reach a bridge (200
feet to the north) you've gone too
far.

The 1826 Round Stone
Barn at Hancock is one
of the best-known symbols
of Shaker skill. Courtesy
Shaker Hancock Village.

HANCOCK SHAKER VILLAGE

"City of Peace"
Pittsfield, Massachusetts
1790-1960

A National Historic Landmark
Famous 1826 Round Stone Barn
Museum, Library, Exhibits, Tours
Educational & Special Programs
Gift Shop & Cafe

A national and state historic landmark, Hancock Shaker Village offers an immaculately restored complex of twenty Church Family buildings set on 1,400 acres in a pretty Berkshire valley.

Once called "City of Peace," it greets the visitor with an air of serenity, the cupola of its well-known Round Stone Barn standing against a skyline of low wooded hills. Its buildings, which were constructed between 1790 and 1916, include the Brick Dwelling, Barns, Workshops, a Meetinghouse, Schoolhouse, Machine Shop/Laundry and even a modernized 1850 Privy from Harvard's South Family, along with other structures.

The Shakers were key consultants in the redevelopment of this village, which was one of the last Shaker communities to close down and one of the first to open as a museum.

The Hancock Collection

At Hancock Shaker Village is the largest documented and representative collection of Shaker artifacts available to the

Hancock Believers worshipping in mid-19th century on their sacred hillside.

public in an original Shaker site. Its furniture, tools and equipment, household objects, textiles, "gift" drawings, and commercial graphics illustrate the Shakers' important place in the social, economic, and religious life of the region during a period of 150 years.

Seventy-five percent of the Village's collection is on exhibit in room settings. Changing gallery exhibits introduce specialized collections to the public. Hancock Shaker Village is a major source of information and loans for researchers and museums in the decorative arts, 19th-century technologies, architecture, communal life, and religion.

The Research Library, located on the second floor of the 1878 Poultry House, has one of the finest collections of Shaker works, archives, and literature about Shaker.

The six families at Hancock were part of a larger community of Shakers in the region. This included Mount Lebanon, in New Lebanon, New York, once the Shaker spiritual and administrative headquarters, just a five-minute drive to the west. Farther west, near Albany, the first Shaker community is at Watervliet in the town of Colonie, less than an hour's drive.

Today, the Shaker Museum in Old Chatham is another point of interest on a Shaker heritage exploration of the region. The Shaker Museum is only twenty miles away, and its collection holds many artifacts that once were part of everyday life in Hancock.

History of the Site

Hancock was the third Shaker community to be established. Believers lived there from 1790-1960. It was one of the longest-lived communities in Shakerdom and the bishopric for two other Shaker villages. Numbering as many as 300 residents in the mid-19th century, Hancock was an important part of the larger community of Shakers in the region. Its long heritage includes personal visits by Mother Ann Lee during the ten years she proselytized in the region in the 1770s-

Courtesy Hancock Shaker Village

View of the Hancock Church Family, 1841.

Simplicity, functionality and quality were the hallmarks of Shaker design. Courtesy Hancock Shaker Village.

Photo: Michael Fredericks

Ministry Kitchen, Hancock. Courtesy Hancock Shaker Village.

1780s. She is said to have preached in a home that once stood near Hancock's Trustees' House.

In its final decades, Hancock took in many elderly Shakers when their original homes in other villages were closed. Eventually, Hancock's last remaining residents grew too old to maintain the community and the Central Shaker Ministry decided to sell the property in 1959 to a local group of Shaker enthusiasts—one of whom was a personal friend of the Shakers. Its buildings then were restored with loving care and an eye to authenticity.

Hancock Shaker Village

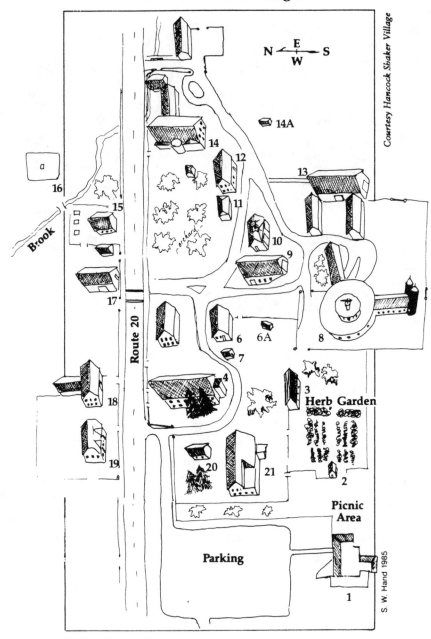

Courtesy Hancock Shaker Village

S. W. Hand 1985

1. Visitor and Village Office
2. Garden Tool Shed
   and Herb Garden
3. Poultry House
   (Library and Exhibit Hall)
4. Brick Dwelling
5. Brethren's Workshop
6. Sisters' Dairy and Weave Shop
6A. Privy
7. Ministry Wash House
8. Round Stone Barn
9. Tan House
10. Ice House
11. Brick Garage
12. Hired Men's Shop/Print Shop
13. 1910-1939 Barn Complex
14. Trustees' Office and Store
14A. Office Privy
15. Schoolhouse
16. Cemetery
17. Horse Barn
18. Ministry Shop
19. Meetinghouse
20. Garage/Wood shed
21. Laundry and Machine Shop

Planning Your Visit

Hancock's modern Visitors' Center and Village Office (1972) offers visitors all the necessary services in one location—restrooms, cafe, information center, and an attractive museum gift shop carrying Shaker and Shaker-related items.

During the main visitation season, one can tour the Brick Dwelling, Round Stone Barn, the Meetinghouse, and the gardens along with a variety of other activities available to visitors who pursue a self-guided walking tour of the Village. In the early and late season, guided tours are given of the most important buildings.

It takes about a half day to tour all the grounds and buildings. Visitors can see the buildings in any order. There are interpreters on the grounds and in the major buildings, available to answer questions. Also available are orientation films, talks, crafts demonstrations, exhibits, etc.

The visitor passes through sheds and workshops, including the Brethren's Workshop, which has room settings that show some of the crafts and trades practiced by the men. The Sisters' Dairy and Weave Shop has a dairy on the first floor and weaving and spinning rooms upstairs.

There is the Tan House (now the Cabinetmaker's Shop and Forge), Ice House, Hired Men's Shop/Print Shop, Cemetery

HANCOCK SHAKER VILLAGE

(reached by a footbridge across a stream), Ministry Shop, and Horse Barn.

The unique Round Stone Barn, built in 1826, is a highlight of the walk. (Animals are kept in a 20th-century addition.) Dairying was a central business at Hancock, and this barn with its innovative design was important to the success of the venture. A brick ell, added to the barn in 1864, houses an exhibit on Shaker agriculture. Of all the Shaker buildings, this massive, beautiful barn probably has been photographed, sketched and painted more than any other.

The 1830 Brick Dwelling once housed almost 100 Shakers. Its symmetry and innovative architectural features reflect the Shaker tenet of separation of the sexes.

Hancock's oldest building is the ca. 1790 Laundry and Machine Shop, which contains early water-powered machinery along with laundry equipment for washing and ironing. The gambrel-roofed 1790s Meetinghouse

Photo: Michael Fredericks

Elders' Room, Hancock. Courtesy Hancock Shaker Village.

contains the original benches where prospective converts or curiosity-seekers of "the World's People" sat to watch the Shakers dance and sing songs of worship on the Sabbath.

The change in Shaker tastes can be seen in the Victorian-style Trustees' Office and Store, which presents a strong contrast to the other buildings. Built to house Trustees, or "office deacons," who handled all business, legal, and financial matters, the Trustees' building is the only surviving example at Hancock of the Shakers' late-19th-century attempts to "modernize."

Most Shaker communities were fairly prosperous when the auto-mobile became the rage in the early part of this century, and the Believers were often known for having the latest and finest automobiles available. Not only did the Believers use trucks for their business and labor, but they enjoyed motoring around the countryside and into the cities, even taking vacations by car. At Hancock, their vehicles were kept in the 1915 four-car Brick Garage—heated with piped-in hot water.

LIVING HISTORY

Hancock is not only a restored Shaker site, but also an "outdoor museum," known for its commitment to "living history." In surrounding fields, crops are grown and animals are raised in the Shaker tradition. Nineteenth-century plant varieties grow in the heirloom vegetable garden.

Between May and October there are many offerings in the way of craft, farm and domestic task workshops, classes, demonstrations and exhibitions of Shaker work.

Documented Shaker techniques in animal husbandry and cultivation are carried out in the gardens, fields and pastures, and historic breeds of cattle, sheep, horses, and chickens help recreate the Village's former agricultural identity. Farm products are used in cooking demonstrations in the authentic 1830s kitchen.

Today, skilled craftspeople in the Hancock workshops use traditional Shaker materials and methods to make reproduction Shaker furniture, baskets, woodenware and textiles. Also, there is a specimen herb garden, which contains plants common to the Shakers' successful medicinal herb industry.

SPECIAL PROGRAMS and Workshops for adults and children are offered throughout the year, and group tours can be arranged with advance reservations.

One such program is "An Evening at Hancock Shaker Village," which includes a guided tour, music program and a candle-light dinner in the Believers' Dining Room with costumed interpreters as hosts. Call for a brochure and menu information.

Among other Hancock events are seasonal farm days and festivals; lectures on Shaker culture; crafts or antiques shows; Christmas programs; and Summertime Discovery Room, with hands-on activities (wool carding, spinning and weaving, old-fashioned toys and games, Shaker-style clothing to try on, schoolroom).

Inquire about pre-registration or reservations. A number of crafts instruction courses are given throughout the year. They may include Shaker basketry, oval boxmaking, chair seat-weaving, joinery or caning, textiles, timber-frame construction, and blacksmithing.

Course fees vary, depending on the materials and time involved.

Tourist Information

Hours: The Village is open daily from 9:30 a.m.-5 p.m., May 1 through October 31. Through the month of April and November 1-30 (excluding Thanksgiving), the Village is open 10 a.m.-3 p.m.

The Research Library is open by appointment. (No admission fee.)

The Museum Shop, which carries an extensive line of reproduction Shaker furniture and kits, is open daily during regular Village hours and into mid-December. Between May and October, the Village Cafe serves snacks and lunch daily. There is a picnic area.

For further site/tour information contact:

Hancock Shaker Village
PO Box 898
Pittsfield, Massachusetts 01202
Tel: 413/443-0188

For additional lodging/dining information contact:

Berkshire Visitors Bureau
Berkshire Common
West Street
Pittsfield, Massachusetts 01201
Tel: 413/443-9186

Access to Hancock

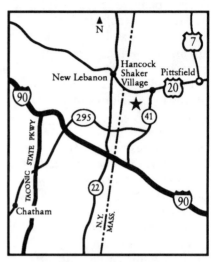

Admission Fee

Limited Handicapped Access

Restrooms

No Pets

Major Credit Cards Accepted

Dining

DIRECTIONS: Hancock Shaker Village is at the junction of Routes 20 and 41, 5 miles west of Pittsfield, Massachusetts, a 45-minute drive from Albany, New York, 1 hour from Springfield, Massachusetts and 2-1/2 to 3 hours from Boston and New York City.

Heading West: From I-90 (Massachusetts Turnpike) take Exit 1. Turn right on Route 41 and follow north to the junction of Route 20. The Village is to the left.

Heading East: It is not possible to get off I-90 at Exit 1. Take Exit B-3 in New York (New York Route 22, New Lebanon/Austerlitz). Follow Route 22 north to the intersection of Route 295. Turn right on 295 and follow it east to the intersection of Route 41. Turn left on 41 and follow it to the intersection of Route 20. The Village is to the left. (Note: Hancock Shaker Village is not located in the Village of Hancock.)

*Church Family Dwelling,
Enfield, Connecticut.
From* Shakerism.

*"All the members of the Church have a just and equal
right to the use of all things, according to their order
and needs..."*

*"Way Works"
By J. Meacham*

ENFIELD

"City of Union"
Enfield, Connecticut
1790-1917

A National Historic District
Birthplace of Father Joseph Meacham
Now a State Prison

Enfield, Connecticut, was the fifth Shaker village to be established. It was "gathered" in 1790, the same year as Hancock, Massachusetts. At its height in 1830, Enfield had approximately 260 Believers living in five Families, on 3,000 acres.

Today, the five remaining Church and North Family buildings are part of a prison, and the remaining South Family buildings are privately owned. Some of the buildings within the prison can be seen from Shaker Road, but permission is needed from the prison if visitors want to stop on the road to view them or the nearby Shaker Cemetery.

The five remaining South Family buildings are listed on the National Register of Historic Places. They have been owned by the Cybulski family for several generations and may be viewed from Cybulski Road. One of these, the thirty-two-room Dwelling House, is the last Shaker Dwelling remaining in Connecticut. There is some concern for this Historic District because of the proposed widening of Cybulski Road to provide additional access to a nearby manufacturing complex, bringing heavy commercial traffic close to the stone foundations of the Shaker buildings.

Late 19th-century stereoptical view of the South Family at Enfield, Connecticut

History of the Site

One of the communities visited by Mother Ann on her 1781 missionary journey, Enfield also was the birthplace of "Father" Joseph Meacham, after Ann Lee perhaps the most important founder of Shakerism. Early Shaker growth depended upon Meacham's remarkable organizational abilities combined with the talents of "Mother" Lucy Wright, who joined him at Mount Lebanon at the end of the 1780s as a spiritual leader of the Shakers.

Father Joseph, formerly a New Light Baptist minister, was Mother Ann's most important convert in America. He suffered persecutions at her side and went on to dynamic leadership during the crucial early years, establishing, organizing, and administering the United Society until he died at Mount Lebanon in 1796.

The world began to take note of the unmistakable Shaker decline when, in 1911, *The New York Times* published "The Last of the Shakers—A Community Awaiting Death." The article was about Enfield, which could count only twenty-two Believers and was described in the *Times* as a "quaint ghostlike colony of religious fanatics." In 1914, the village was sold, and three years later, the last Believers departed.

After Enfield closed, most buildings were acquired by the state in 1931 and turned into Osborn State Prison Farm. For forty-six years, until 1977, it was operated as a dairy farm in order to provide vocational training to inmates. With the prisoner population being mostly city-bred by then the state closed up the farm and sold the prison's herd at auction.

In 1876 the Enfield community had built a large new Dwelling House. It was, according to *Shakerism*, "a fine, commodious brick edifice, equipped with every modern convenience and containing a beautiful library, a music room and a chapel." Since being taken over by the state in 1931, the 1876 Dwelling has been torn down, one among almost seventy Shaker structures which have disappeared from the site. The small West and East Families, closed in the mid-19th

Courtesy Hancock Shaker Village

Sisters and children at Enfield, Connecticut about the turn of the century. The original is at Old Chatham Shaker Museum and Library.

Rug weaving at Enfield, Connecticut.

century, have no remaining buildings. All that is left of the more than fifty North and Church Families' buildings within the prison walls are the Ox Barn, Cart Shed, Colt Shed and hired man's house of the North Family and the third Meetinghouse and Elder George Wilcox's shop of the Church Family.

The South Family once had twenty buildings. Among the few privately owned structures remaining are: the Dwelling and Wash House, Dairy, Grain Barn, Shop, Ice House and Privy.

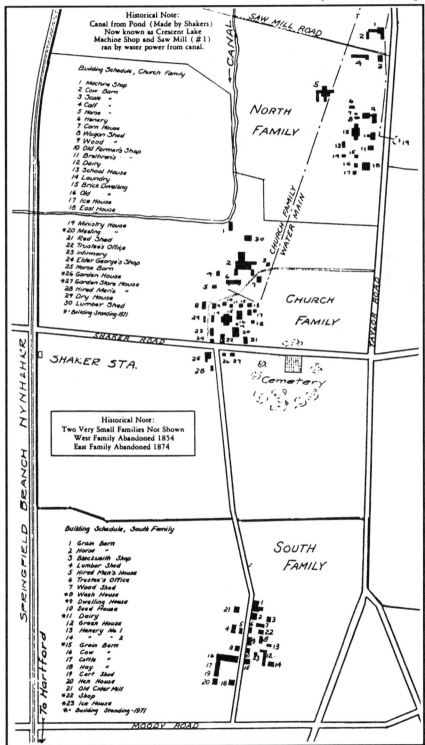

Enfield in the late 19th century.

Planning Your Visit

Permission to stop on the roadside and view the buildings is needed from the prison supervisor. While tours can be arranged with the prison administration from time to time, visitation is restricted. Write or call the Enfield Historical Society which acts as a conduit for visitor requests.

Those houses south of Shaker Road which are privately owned by the Cybulskis may be viewed without advance permission. Cybulski Road is a dead end which can be entered from Moody Road. (Please respect the owners' property rights and privacy.)

The Enfield Historical Society is a key site interpreter for Enfield. It has a Shaker room with artifacts from Enfield, and a number of large Shaker artifacts displayed elsewhere in the museum, including a late 19th-century Shaker Hearse, some of the Enfield washroom tubs, and cupboards, a bell from the Church Family Dwelling, and an interior paneled wall from the Seed House.

Tourist Information

Hours: The Historical Society is open every Sunday 1-4:30 p.m., from the first Sunday in May to the last Sunday in October, and by appointment.

For further site information contact:

Enfield Historical Society
1294 Enfield Street (Route 5)
Enfield, Connecticut 06082
Tel: (203) 745-1724

For lodging/dining information contact:

North Central Connecticut Convention & Visitor's Bureau
111 Hazard Avenue
Enfield, Connecticut 06082
Tel: 203/763-2578 or
    800/248-8283

Courtesy Cybulski Family

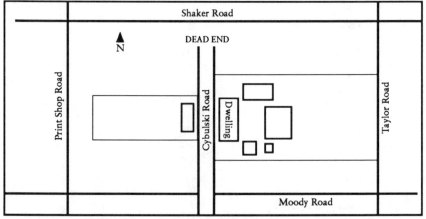

Present-day site map of Enfield, showing remaining South Family buildings.

Access to Enfield

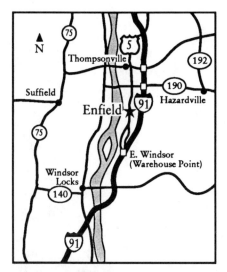

DIRECTIONS: The Enfield site is 4 miles east of Thompsonville in the Town of Enfield. From I-91, take exit for Route 190. At the first fork in the road, take the left onto Shaker Road.

To reach Enfield Historical Society Museum from the Shaker site, take Shaker Road (Route 220) west (it becomes Elm Street) to Enfield Street (Route 5). Turn south onto Enfield. The museum is 1.5 miles on the right in the Old Town Hall, a large white building. (Note: Several blocks south of here, Puritan minister Jonathan Edwards delivered his famous sermon "Sinners in the Hands of an Angry God" during the Great Awakening. A stone marks the site.)

*Entrance to Hoyt Nurseries,
former home of the New Canaan
Shaker community. From the
1867 F.W. Beers, Atlas of New
York and Vicinity.*

NEW CANAAN

New Canaan, Connecticut
1810-1812

Nothing remains and little is known about this short-lived community. Its site is now a housing development, and local historians cannot offer an exact location for its buildings.

According to one of the best sources of information, "Zion on Clapboard Hill," by Gerard C. Wertkin, published in the *New Canaan Historical Society Annual,* 1979-80, the Village was begun early in 1810, during a time of rapid expansion for the Shakers. The Shaker leaders at New Lebanon purchased 130 acres of land in the town of New Canaan from Stephen Fitch, a new convert and prosperous local resident.

On the land were two houses, two barns and several outbuildings on a site called Clapboard Hill. The facing page illustration shows, on the left, one of the houses the Shakers purchased in 1810. It burned down in 1881, along with the outbuildings shown. The location was not far from Long Island Sound, suitable as a place for invalid Believers to recuperate. It became the home for a dozen New Lebanon Believers—several prominent in the public ministry—who moved there that spring.

History of the Site

Work on the stony land was difficult, and many a stone wall was built from the clearing of the fields. However, there was little interest in the faith from Connecticut residents and only three conversions. Although few Shakers lived there, at least eighty-five visited the site in the two years of its existence.

In the meantime, Fitch left the novitiate order a year later after demanding payment in full for the land and becoming estranged from the Shaker leaders. One Shaker wrote "We want no more of him," and others called him a "devil." Controversy between Fitch and the Believers continued, as he removed two of his three sons from the community at New Lebanon. The third son disobeyed him and remained.

The high lump-sum costs involved in purchasing the site and building a granary, combined with the hardship of working the land, convinced the Shaker leaders to sell the property. By spring, 1812, the community was sold and the New Canaan Shakers returned to New Lebanon, "probably not without considerable regret," writes Wertkin.

A troublesome aspect of the endeavor was the ongoing conflict with Stephen Fitch, who reappeared at Mount Lebanon from time to time and behaved disagreeably. At one point, he even brought his two sons back to Mount Lebanon, demanding that the Society care for them.

The New Canaan site—for years known as "Shaker Farm"—became part of New Canaan Nurseries (or Hoyt Nursery) from 1848 until 1970. With its 800 acres, it was the largest tree nursery in the state. In 1970 it was sold to RCA, which resold over 200 acres for residential development.

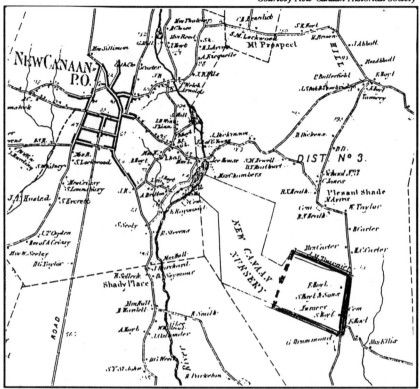

Section of 1867 map, showing the town of New Canaan in Fairfield County, Connecticut. The Shaker community is outlined at bottom right.

This 1867 map shows the approximate location of the Shaker land within the bounds of the "New Canaan Nursery." Not all this land was Shaker, for the Hoyts expanded their nursery more than six times over the original Shaker land purchase. The road bounding the east (right) side of the site (with dots marking Hoyt residences) marks the approximate location of the Shaker structures. The dot for "S. Hoyt" marks the house that burned in 1881.

Planning Your Visit

The Shaker site is now private property transversed by several new country roads, and nothing marks the location of the site. Information on the community is widely scattered, as references in Wertkin's above-mentioned article indicate.

For research or general information about the New Canaan Shakers, contact the New Canaan Historical Society Museum and Library, which has several files of Shaker material.

Tourist Information

Museum and Library
Hours: Tuesday through Saturday 9:30 a.m.-12:30 p.m. and 2-4:30 p.m. Research by appointment.

For further site information contact:

New Canaan Historical Society
13 Oenoke Ridge
New Canaan, Connecticut 06840
Tel: 203/966-1776

For lodging/dining information contact:

Yankee Heritage District
297 West Avenue
Norwalk, Connecticut 06850
Tel: 203/854-7825

Access to New Canaan

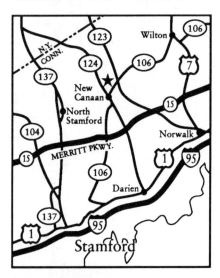

DIRECTIONS: To reach the New Canaan Historical Society, take Exit 17 off the Merritt Parkway; turn left onto Route 124; go 2.5 miles to Museum and Library, on the left.

Looking across the Tannery
Pond at the Meetinghouse
in Mount Lebanon.

MOUNT LEBANON

"Holy Mount"
New Lebanon, New York
1787-1947

A National Historic Landmark
Exhibits, Educational Programming
Guided or Self-Guided Tour
Gift Shop

Mount Lebanon Shaker Village, once the most sacred place in all Shakerdom, is listed on the National Register of Historic Places. Located in a beautiful hillside setting in rural New Lebanon, New York, the Village even today recalls a statement by a visitor in 1867 who said, "Mount Lebanon strikes you as a place where it is always Sunday."

Known by the spiritual name "Holy Mount," Mount Lebanon is of foremost importance in America's Shaker heritage, in part because it was the model from which all other villages were developed. It is also important because it was the spiritual and administrative center of Shakerdom until 1947.

Of the approximately forty remaining buildings at the site, twenty-six from the North, Church and Center Families are owned and administered by the nonprofit corporation, Mount Lebanon Shaker Village.

The rest of the buildings, from the Second and South Families, are privately owned and not open to the public, but many can be seen from the outside on a walking tour. The

Shaker Circle Dance at Mount Lebanon. From Frank Leslie's Popular Monthly, XX (December, 1885) No. 6.

Mount Lebanon, with North Family in the foreground. From Charles Edson Robinson's The Shakers.

Village shows a wide-ranging architectural diversity, and its structures often were prototypes for construction in other Shaker communities. Several in the North Family are open to the public.

Mount Lebanon is one of three major Shaker points of interest within a short distance of one another: Hancock Shaker Village is a few miles to the east, and the Shaker Museum and Library is a twenty-minute drive to the southwest in Old Chatham.

History of Site

When in 1787 the early Believers first "gathered in gospel order," Mount Lebanon was their main community, where they had built their first Meetinghouse in 1785. For more than 150 years Mount Lebanon housed the Central Ministry of Shakerdom.

This ministry established church doctrine and government and models for agriculture, manufacturing, handicrafts, and architecture. It decided on all important matters, including religious practices and doctrine, expansion of Shakerdom, community development, major expenditures, business ventures, and publishing.

At its height in the mid-19th century, the Mount Lebanon society numbered 600 persons and owned more than 6,000 acres. Mount Lebanon was looked to for guidance by Believers in communities as far away as Busro, Indiana, during the early 19th-century expansion, and south to Florida late in that century. Its role as headquarters ended by 1947, when the Society at Mount Lebanon was closed.

Repurchased for Preservation

When, in the 1930s and 1940s, the Shaker trustees began to sell off Mount Lebanon buildings, most of the Church Family property went to a private boarding school which is now

Courtesy Mount Lebanon Shaker Village

A Sister in the North Family dooryard at Mount Lebanon about the turn of the century. From Shakerism.

The Office and Store at Mount Lebanon. From Harper's New Monthly Magazine, No. LXXXVI, July, 1857.

A portrait of Mount Lebanon Shakers late in the 19th century.

General view of the Second Meetinghouse from the southeast as it stands today.

named for David Darrow, a leading early Shaker whose farm-land this had been in the late 18th century. Other buildings were bought in their family groups, including the South Family buildings, which currently belong to Sufis, a religious group.

In 1991, thanks to the help of a grant from the State of New York, most of the Mount Lebanon buildings were purchased from the Darrow School by the Mount Lebanon Shaker Village, assuring future preservation and eventual restoration of the buildings. Darrow School now leases back many of the buildings. The students at the school take part in a "Hands to Work Class," which involves keeping the grounds groomed.

Ongoing (as it will be for many years to come) is essential stabilization and repair work in a number of buildings. Because of the great cost of this work, the Shaker Village is

The remains of the North Family Stone Barn, which burned down in the mid-1970s, still stand as a testimony to Shaker construction.

moving slowly but making steady progress in those most critical and fundamental of preservation labors—shoring up, repairing foundations, and making roofs and walls watertight.

In general, most buildings at Mount Lebanon have been maintained by the private owners who, over the years, have shown respect for the Shaker legacy. One example is the North Family Granary, occupied by a craftsman who makes reproduction Shaker furniture using methods employed by the Shakers. It also serves as the Village gift shop and furniture showroom.

Through the years there have been tragic losses, the most notable being the burning down of the mammoth North Family Stone Barn in 1972. The foundation still stands, attesting to the community's former prosperity, and there are hopes of one day building on it again.

Courtesy Mount Lebanon Shaker Village

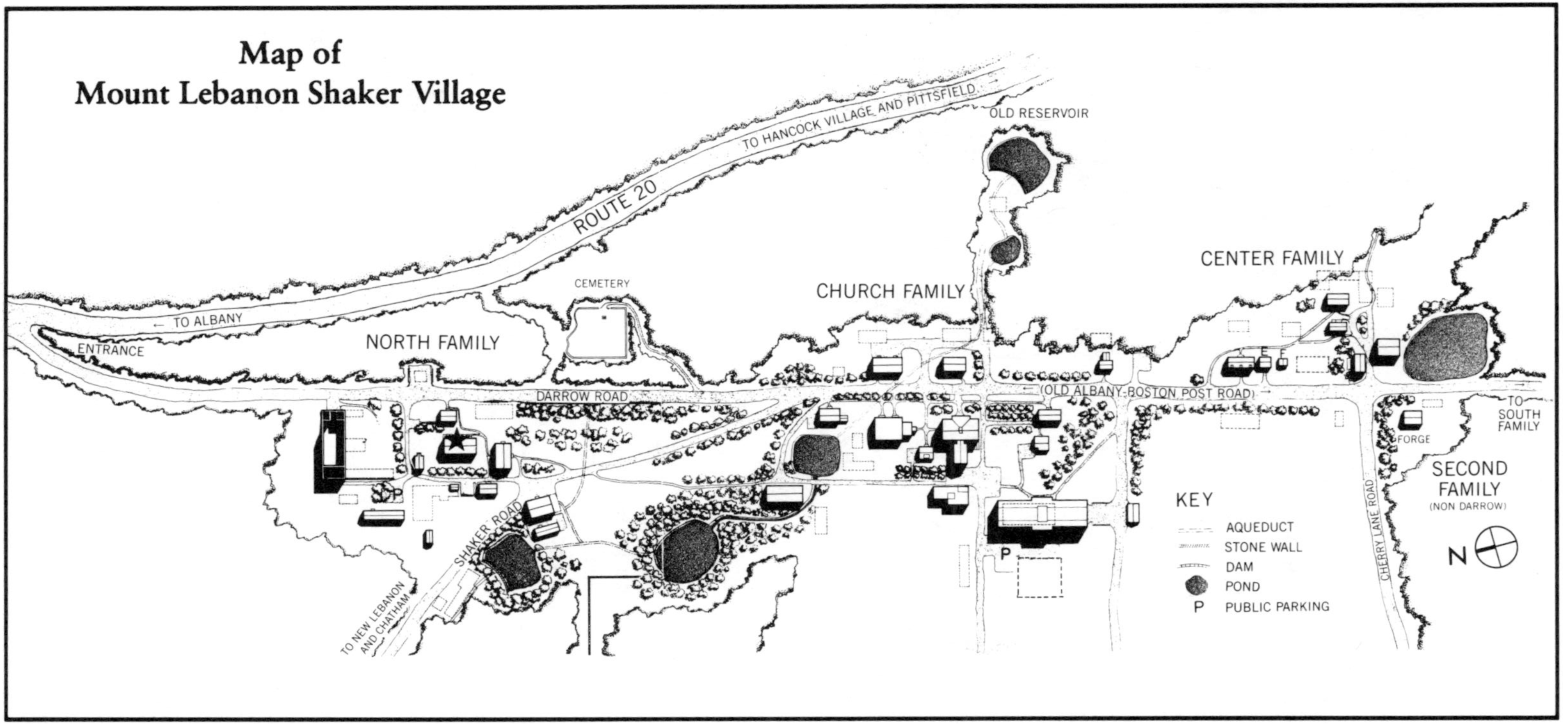

Map of
Mount Lebanon Shaker Village
ROUTE 20
TO HANCOCK VILLAGE AND PITTSFIELD
← TO ALBANY
ENTRANCE
NORTH FAMILY
CEMETERY
OLD RESERVOIR
CHURCH FAMILY
CENTER FAMILY
DARROW ROAD
(OLD ALBANY-BOSTON POST ROAD)
SHAKER ROAD
TO NEW LEBANON AND CHATHAM
P
TO SOUTH FAMILY
FORGE
SECOND FAMILY
(NON DARROW)
CHERRY LANE ROAD
KEY
AQUEDUCT
STONE WALL
DAM
POND
P PUBLIC PARKING
N

Planning Your Visit

Photo: Golden Hill Press

The buildings open to the public include the North Family Wash House, the North Family Brethren's Workshop, the Plant Nursery and the Granary. Also, an exhibit can be viewed in the foyer of the Church Family Meetinghouse, which serves as the Darrow School library.

The best way to see the Village is on foot, and a booklet describing a walking tour of the community can be acquired at the Visitor's Center, where the walk starts. A slide show can be viewed and guides are available to take visitors on tours, or you may go on your own if you desire. (Since various kinds of construction work are ongoing, visitors are alerted to use good judgment, especially with children, in places where there might be hazards.)

The walking tour leads from the North Family Wash House to the 1818 Dwelling House foundation, which once housed the North Family. This building had to be razed in 1973, and its doors,

The Mount Lebanon Visitor Center.

windows, pegboards, chair railings, etc., are now part of the New York Metropolitan Museum of Art's "Shaker Room" exhibit.

Other buildings on the walk are: the 1852 Sisters' Shop and Store; the 1838 Granary; the foundation of the 1858 Stone Barn (said to have been the largest stone barn in the western hemisphere); the Spruce Tree, planted by the Shakers and seen in old photographs; the ca. 1860 Carriage House or Wagon Shed; the ca. 1860 Plant Nursery and Herb Gardens; the early 19th-century foundation of the Saw and Grist Mill; the 1855 Stone Dam; the 1829 Brethren's Workshop, a brick building which houses the village office, exhibit galleries and artifact storage; the 1849 Forge, now leased as a private residence; and the North Family Kitchen Garden.

Also on the walking tour: the ca. 1835 West House; the ca. 1840 Farm Deacon's Shop; the Shaker Community Memorial which stands at the site of the North and Church Family burials (1856-1948) but is presently almost inaccessible to visitors because of a difficult slope; the 1838 Tannery, now used as the Darrow School chapel and for chamber concerts; and the 1785 First Meetinghouse, the first building erected by the Shakers to serve specifically as a meetinghouse, which later was moved to serve as the Schoolhouse, then the Seed House.

Next is the 1824 Second Meetinghouse, with a striking barrel or "rainbow" roof, which houses the Darrow library; the 1876 Ministry House or Shop; the 1876 Church Family Dwelling House, housing Darrow administrative offices; the 1827 Trustees' Office and Store; the 1857 Infirmary; the 1826 Church Family Brethren's Workshop; the Dairy or Milk House, perhaps the oldest structure in the Village, having been part of the original David Darrow farm; and the 1839 Schoolhouse.

At the site of the Center Family can be seen: the Ann Lee Cottage, erected in 1825, named in honor of Mother Ann and the first Dwelling House of the Center Family; the Cherry Lane Cottage, once used as a processing workshop in the herb and medicinal industry, for which the Shakers were well known; the Sheep Barn; the 1864 Valentine Cottage, believed to have been the pharmacy; the Medicine Shop, once part of a complex of buildings that housed the medicinal production, but which has been razed; and the 1846 limestone Forge.

Mount Lebanon has an enormous labyrinth of reservoirs, ponds, sluices, pipes, conduits, springs, and brooks created to bring fresh water to houses, shops, and farms. This progressive and unique aqueduct system is being studied for eventual rehabilitation.

Part of the site's future development will include nature trails and outside exhibits, integrated with the walking tour as an historic park. This plan includes replanting vegetable gardens, rebuilding fences and walls, and restoring the remarkable system of water delivery and storage.

The privately owned South Family and Second Family buildings are beyond the southern end of the site. Visitors are requested not to impinge on the privacy of these residences. Ask the staff for specific information about these buildings—one of which Mother Ann stayed in when she came to Mount Lebanon.

SPECIAL PROGRAMS

Educational programs, workshops, events, and lectures take place throughout the season; these include week-long Elderhostel programs and guided hikes to Holy Mount, the consecrated holy ground of Mount Lebanon Shakers. There are also archaeology sessions, sketching and photography instruction, ornithology walks, basketmaking, and boxmaking.

In late spring is Herb Day, when plants may be purchased and their use explained; there are also weekends of Shaker craft demonstrations and sheep-shearing and various events held in conjunction with the "I Love New York" Fall Festival in Columbia County.

Other programs are offered from time to time during the season. Call for information.

Tourist Information

Hours: Memorial Day weekend to Labor Day weekend, 9:30 a.m.-5 p.m. daily; through October 31, Friday through Sunday; November 1 to Memorial Day, by appointment.

Museum Store: Open during season; no admission charge for store visit only.

For further site/tour information contact:
Mount Lebanon Shaker Village
PO Box 628
New Lebanon, New York 12125
Tel: 518/794-9500

For additional lodging/dining information contact:

Columbia County Tourism
401 State Street
Hudson, New York 12534
Tel: 800/777-9247 or
518/828-3375

Berkshire Visitors Bureau
Berkshire Common
West Street
Pittsfield, Massachusetts 01201
Tel: 413/443-9186

Admission Fee   Limited Handicapped Access   Restrooms   No Pets in Buildings

Major Credit Cards For Gift Shop Only

Access to Mt. Lebanon

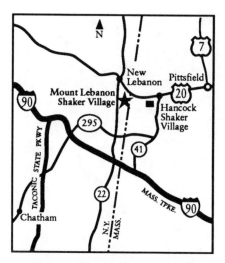

DIRECTIONS: Mount Lebanon Shaker Village is in New Lebanon, New York, on Route 20, 11 miles west of Pittsfield, Massachusetts, and less than an hour from Albany, New York, to the west. It can be reached from I-90 by taking the Route 22 exit and traveling north on Route 22 to New Lebanon; at the flashing light, make a right and drive 2 miles east on Route 20. As you head up the mountain, look for the "Darrow School" and "Mount Lebanon Shaker Village" signs on the right.

Photo: Paul Rocheleau

Bottles and vat for the
medicinal herb industry.
Courtesy The Shaker
Museum and Library.

SHAKER MUSEUM AND LIBRARY

Old Chatham, New York

World's Largest Shaker Collection
Museum, Library, Exhibits
Educational & Special Programs
Self-Guided Tours, Gift Shop, Summer Kitchen

Surrounded by beautiful rolling countryside, the Shaker Museum and Library in Old Chatham, New York, is for Shaker enthusiasts an essential and immeasurably rewarding destination. There are more than 17,000 objects in the Museum buildings and 18,000 items in the Library. The combined collection ranges from precious "gift" drawings and original manuscripts of Shaker manifestoes to a massive, seven-ton, double trip-hammer that looks as serviceable today as when used at Mount Lebanon in 1820.

Other proofs of Shaker inventive genius in this, the largest collection of Shaker artifacts and writings, are a horse-drawn fire engine from Canterbury, New Hampshire; a tongue and groove (woodworking joint) machine, invented by Shakers in 1828 and the patented washing machine from Canterbury that won a gold medal at the Philadelphia Centennial Exposition in 1876.

The Shaker Museum and Library's interpretive exhibitions not only include a wide variety of manufactured items, but also the tools, patterns, and machinery used to make them: oval boxes, baskets, buckets, and stoves share galleries and exhibition space with broom- and chair-making equip-

Photo: Paul Rocheleau

The Shaker Museum displays many examples of Shaker inventiveness including a seven ton double trip-hammer originally from Mount Lebanon, New York, (above); a horse-drawn fire engine from Canterbury, New Hampshire; the first tongue and groove machine invented in 1828; and a patented washing machine from Canterbury that won a Gold Medal at the Philadelphia Centennial Exposition in 1876. Courtesy The Shaker Museum and Library.

ment, woodworking tools and benches, cloaks and the patterns to shape them and the wardrobes in which to keep them, medicine room chests of drawers and work tables, garden seeds, pharmaceuticals, and sewing, spinning, and weaving implements.

In 1993 the Charles and Helen Upton Collection was created with 215 objects from one of the greatest private collections. It has three components: the study collection, of 180 objects including the range of Shaker material culture; thirty-five masterpieces reflecting Shaker's highest achievement; and seven linear feet of archival records enhancing understanding of Shaker life in the 20th century.

A full-time librarian manages a modern system that enables researchers to survey Shaker Museum and Library holdings in a matter of minutes. The collections of both

Photo: Paul J. Rocheleau

An exhibit gallery in the museum. Courtesy The Shaker Museum and Library.

Photo: Golden Hill Press

The Shaker Museum and Library at Old Chatham.

Library and Museum are cataloged and inventoried in an encyclopedic resource system.

History of the Site

The Shaker Museum and Library was founded by John S. Williams, Sr., who worked with Eldress Emma Neale of Mount Lebanon and Eldress Emma B. King of Canterbury to create a public museum which would preserve the Shaker legacy. In addition to the thousands of objects purchased by Williams, primarily from Mount Lebanon, over 500 donors contributed to the collections. The Shaker Museum opened to the public in 1950 with a charter from the New York State Board of Regents.

Williams was a Long Island financier whose farm in Columbia County was not far from Mount Lebanon. He had begun to collect Shaker artifacts in 1935 and opened the Shaker Museum with approximately 4,000 objects. Through the 1950s he adapted his farm buildings one after another to accommodate what was gathered. Along with its library, named after Eldress Emma B. King, the Museum preserves 200 years of Shaker history. The Shaker Museum and Library has been accredited by the American Association of Museums since 1972.

Photo: Golden Hill Press

The museum is housed in a former dairy farm complex.

Planning Your Visit

Along with over twenty exhibition galleries, visitors may experience a variety of lectures, workshops, and demonstrations.

Educational programs include a comprehensive schedule of educational and instructional offerings throughout most of the year. The centerpiece of this program is found in the Shaker Museum and Library's Education Center, where a variety of temporary exhibitions also are presented.

A sampling of educational programming:

- The John S. Williams, Sr. Lecture Series with presentations by scholars of Shaker history.
- Genealogy workshops, using resources of the Library and suggesting ways to determine if a Shaker relation is in one's family.
- Workshops in Shaker Studies that place the Shaker experience within the wider context of American culture.
- Exhibits of materials from the Emma B. King Library with related lectures on Shaker architecture.
- Formal and informal discussions related to the collection.
- Children's programming, such as crafts, entertainment for the family, and encouragement for children in experiencing and appreciating a museum.

SPECIAL PROGRAMS
The site hosts an Herb Fair and Plant Sale on the Sunday of Memorial Day weekend; a Strawberry Shortcake Breakfast on July 4th; and an Antiques Festival on the first Saturday in August; and Autumn Apple Special, a six-week promotion in September and October.

Tourist Information

Hours: Exhibition buildings are open daily, 10 a.m.-5 p.m., May 1-October 31; the Emma B. King Library is open year-round by appointment.

Museum Shop and Summer Kitchen cafe: open during the season; visitors who wish to go only to the shop or cafe may acquire a free pass at the information office.

Access to Old Chatham

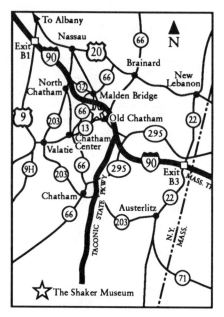

The Shaker Museum

From Albany and New York State Thruway, north and west: Take I-90 to exit 11E, and turn right onto U.S. 20; turn right onto Route 66 south, near Brainard. At Malden Bridge turn left onto Shaker Museum Road.

For further site/tour information contact:

The Shaker Museum & Library
Old Chatham, New York 12136
Tel: 518/794-9100

For additional lodging/dining information contact:

Columbia County Tourism
401 State Street
Hudson, New York 12534
Tel: 800/777-9247 or
    518/828-3375

Berkshire Visitors Bureau
Berkshire Common
West Street
Pittsfield, Massachusetts 01201
Tel: 413/443-9186

DIRECTIONS: The Shaker Museum and Library is just a few minutes from the Taconic State Parkway and the New York State Thruway, 1 mile south of the hamlet of Old Chatham, off County Route 13, on Shaker Museum Road.

From New York City and south: take the Taconic Parkway north to Route 295 exit; turn right onto Route 295; turn left at East Chatham Post Office.; at Old Chatham, left on County Route 13, 1 mile to Shaker Museum Road on the right.

From Boston and east: take the Massachusetts Turnpike (I-90) to B2 exit; turn left onto Route 295; follow above directions.

Admission Fee | Limited Handicapped Access | Restrooms | No Pets

Major Credit Cards Accepted Gift Shop Only | Dining

Photo: Golden Hill Press

MOTHER
ANN LEE
BORN IN MANCHESTER
ENGLAND.
FEB. 29, 1736.
DIED IN WATERVLIET N.Y.
SEPT. 8, 1784.

*The grave of Mother Ann,
in the Shaker Cemetery,
Watervliet, New York*

WATERVLIET

"Wisdom's Valley"
Colonie, New York
1776-1938

> *A National Historic District*
> *Grave of Mother Ann*
> *Guided and Self-Guided Tours*
> *Special Programs*

America's first Shaker settlement was originally known by the Indian name "Niskayuna." Except for her 1781-1783 missionary journeys, this community was the home of Mother Ann Lee from 1776-1784. Eight buildings remain at the Church Family site, as the Shaker Heritage Society and a county facility. The remaining South and West Family buildings are privately owned.

Though Mother Ann never lived in any of the existing 19th-century buildings—her first cottage stood about 500 yards north of the present site—Watervliet always had a special meaning for the Shakers because of her connection to it.

The unpretentious Shaker graveyard here is a particular point of interest for those who want to visit the most significant sites in Shakerdom: Mother Ann and other important early Believers are buried here.

Watervliet, in the Town of Colonie, is within an hour's drive of Mount Lebanon, Hancock Village, and the Old Chatham Shaker Museum and Library across the Hudson River to the east.

Much is now being done to preserve the present Watervliet site, which is now made up of the remaining Church

Photo: Golden Hill Press

The Museum at Watervliet, New York is in the 1848 Meetinghouse.

Family buildings. (Other buildings remaining from the South and West Families are privately owned.) Since 1977 there has been an active local association, known as the Shaker Heritage Society, to keep alive the memory and the traditions of the Shakers. The nonprofit society has offices, exhibits, and a gift shop in the 1848 Meetinghouse.

History of the Site

This community was a thriving Shaker village from its inception in 1776 right through the 19th century, although Mount Lebanon remained the spiritual and organizational focus of the Society.

Mother Ann and other Shakers were living in Watervliet during the Revolution when they were accused of being British loyalists and imprisoned. Confined in Albany and Poughkeepsie jails for almost six months in 1780, Mother Ann was granted her release on the condition that she not speak in public against the war.

Private Collection

Examples of mid-19th century Shaker costume. From Harper's New Monthly Magazine, No. LXXXVI, July, 1857. Harper Brothers Publishers, New York.

It was from her primitive log cottage here that Mother Ann set out in May of 1781 for the two-year pilgrimage throughout New England that laid the foundation for the "gathering" of the Shakers. It was to Watervliet that she returned from that difficult missionary journey in September of 1783. She died there a year later.

Once there were four families totaling as many as 500 persons here, on 700 acres with at least eighty structures. The Watervliet Church Family property was sold in 1924; acquired by Albany County two years later, the buildings were incorporated into a geriatric nursing facility now known as the Ann Lee Home. The remainder of the Shaker community located at the South Family did not finally close its doors until 1938, its loss a sadly symbolic scene of the final act in the story of Shaker decline. Some buildings, privately owned, survived from the South and West Families. Most North Family buildings were destroyed in a fire in the 1920s. None remain and the site is now The Shaker Ridge Country Club.

Watervliet, New York Meetinghouse, mid-19th century. From Shakerism.

Today, Watervliet is hemmed in by an expanding county airport, and a few feet from a minor-league baseball park is Mother Ann's grave in a modest cemetery. This is one of the few Shaker burying grounds with single white headstones, 445 of them rank upon rank. Mother Ann's stone is the highest, standing out from the rest. Originally interred in another graveyard, on land which did not belong to the Society, her remains were moved here in 1835. Other founders who lie near her are Father William Lee (her brother) and Mother Lucy Wright, an important leader who directed the Shakers' western expansion in the early 19th century.

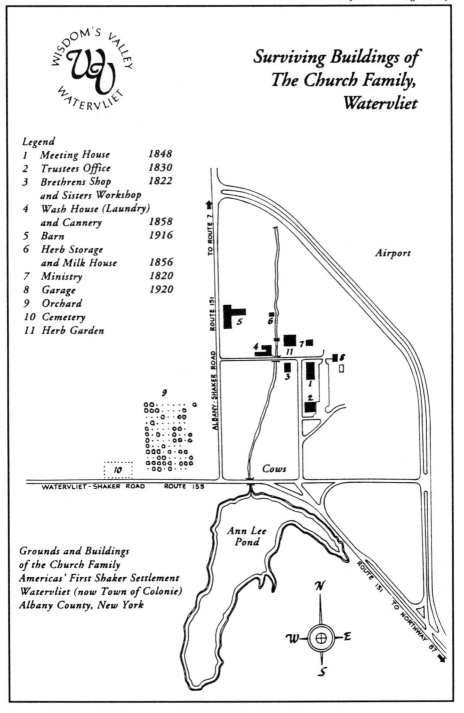

Surviving Buildings of
The Church Family,
Watervliet

Legend
1 Meeting House   1848
2 Trustees Office   1830
3 Brethrens Shop   1822
   and Sisters Workshop
4 Wash House (Laundry)
   and Cannery   1858
5 Barn   1916
6 Herb Storage
   and Milk House   1856
7 Ministry   1820
8 Garage   1920
9 Orchard
10 Cemetery
11 Herb Garden

Grounds and Buildings
of the Church Family
Americas' First Shaker Settlement
Watervliet (now Town of Colonie)
Albany County, New York

Planning Your Visit

The 1848 Church Family Meeting-house houses a museum and gift shop. The building itself is the major exhibit. The museum has exhibits explaining Shaker origins, the Watervliet site, worship practices within the Meetinghouse and Shaker textiles.

The other seven buildings of the Church Family are seen from the outside on the walking tour, for which a brochure is available. Guided group tours are offered by appointment. These can include craft demonstrations and work-shops. The Milk House can be opened for group tours. The gift shop has Shaker reproductions—boxes, baskets, furnishings—books, and children's items.

Still intact are the cemetery and orchard. The Herb Garden is planted within the foundation outline of the Sisters' Workshop and has samples of over eighty-five medicinal herbs grown, used or sold by the Watervliet Shakers. The walking tour of the Church Family begins in the 1848 Meetinghouse and proceeds to the 1830 Trustees' Office, the 1822 Brethren's Shop, and the Sisters' Workshop. Next are the Wash House and Cannery (both 1858) and a relatively modern (1916) Barn; the Herb Storage and Milk House (1856), Ministry Shop (1820), and Garage (1920) are also on the tour.

Not every building that can be seen on the walking tour is accessi-ble to the public, some being used

SHAKER HERITAGE SOCIETY

as county facilities. A number of surviving Shaker buildings from the South and West families are still standing. Visitors to the site can ask for directions to find them, though they are privately owned and not open to the public. Please respect the owners' privacy.

SPECIAL PROGRAMS

Educational and cultural program-ming and demonstrations are held year-round. Several annual events have been established, including a "Learning Fair" geared for fourth graders; more than 2,000 of them come to the site during the first week in May. In a field there are several Black Angus heifers from spring to fall, an attraction for chil-dren who visit the site. An Antiques Show is held the first Saturday in June, a Shaker Reproduction Show in September, and a juried Craft Show in October.

Tourist Information

Hours: Year-round (except major holidays), Tuesday-Friday, noon-4 p.m. Gift shop open Monday-Friday, 10 a.m.-4 p.m., some Saturdays. Group tours (over ten persons) by appointment.

For further site/tour information contact:

Shaker Heritage Society
1848 Shaker Meetinghouse
Albany-Shaker Road
Albany, New York 12211
Tel: 518/456-7890

For lodging/dining information contact:

Albany County Convention & Visitors Bureau
52 Pearl Street
Albany, New York 12207
Tel: 800/258-3582 or
    518/434-1217

Access to Watervliet

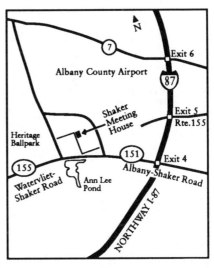

Admission
Fee

Limited
Handicapped
Access

Restrooms

Pets
Permitted
Outside
Only

No
Credit Cards
Accepted

DIRECTIONS: Watervliet can be reached from Exit 4 of the Northway (I-87); go west 1.3 miles on Albany-Shaker Road; stay straight at stop sign onto the grounds of the Ann Lee Home. The second building on the right is the Shaker Meetinghouse.

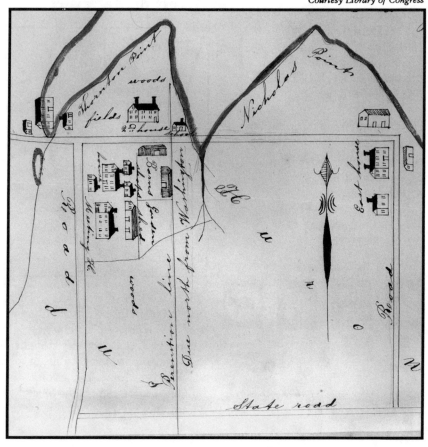

*1835 view of Sodus Shaker
Village by George Kendall
(after Isaac Youngs, July 1834).*

SODUS BAY
Towns of Sodus & Huron, New York
1826-1836

Guided Tours & Special Events

In 1826 land was bought by the Shakers to establish the order's 20th community. On Lake Ontario, thirty miles east of Rochester, Sodus Bay was "a beautiful sheet of water, with level, rolling lands of a deep, rich soil on the southern shore," according to *Shakerism*. Today, part of the tract is a development of modern homes and the rest a large farm. Of the twelve structures built by the Shakers, only three remain: the Church Family Dwelling, Deacon's House or Shop, and a barn.

Sodus Bay was the largest natural harbor on the American side of the lake, and just twelve miles north of the Erie Canal, promising the Shakers economic success for the future. The Sodus group was well-established and prospering when, in the 1830s, plans were announced for another canal, to be built through the land of the Believers. There seemed little choice for the Shakers but to depart rather than have their community surrounded by the development that inevitably followed canal routes.

In 1836, the Sodus community bought land at Groveland, about ninety miles southwest. The following year the Believers sadly left the rich work of their hands at Sodus Bay—more than 1,300 timbered and open acres, with bountiful orchards and productive fields.

No canal ever was built to Sodus Bay, and the speculative purchasers of the Shaker land eventually went bankrupt. The Olean Canal did, ironically, snake its way into the new site at Groveland and proved to be a boon for Shaker business there.

History of the Site

At Sodus, the eastern part of the Shaker tract was in the Town of Port Bay (renamed Huron in 1843) and the western part in the Town of Sodus. The community never numbered

Map: Golden Hill Press

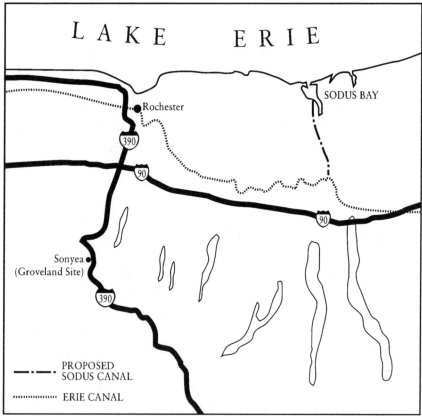

Map showing Sodus in relation to Erie Canal, proposed canal, and Groveland.

more than 150 at one time, but in this period there was a lively proselytizing work going on, with many interested persons attending the public worship services, and some joining the community. Herbert Wisbey's monograph notes that sixty per cent of those who entered the society in its twelve years at Sodus Bay left again.

At Sodus there were four major families in at least thirty-five buildings, served by a meetinghouse that was built in 1831. This building was destroyed by fire in 1925.

The Dwelling of the Church Family, built in 1834, still stands as the main house of Alasa Farms, established by Alvah Griffin Strong of Rochester who purchased the Shaker property in 1924. In 1962, Strong sold that part of the farm in the Town of Huron to the developer of a subdivision that became Shaker Heights. The rest of the formerly Shaker property, with the remaining barn and shop, is still in private hands and continues as part of the working farm.

Courtesy Alasa Farms

Church Family Dwelling House built in 1833-34. The building is now the manor house of Alasa Farms.

Courtesy Alasa Farms

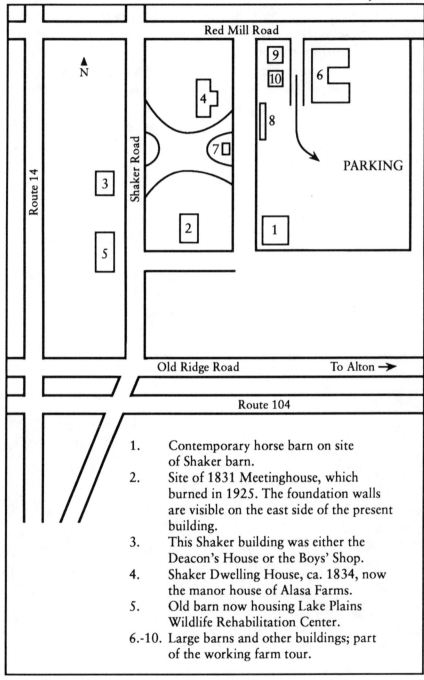

Contemporary Site Map of Sodus, New York.

1. Contemporary horse barn on site of Shaker barn.
2. Site of 1831 Meetinghouse, which burned in 1925. The foundation walls are visible on the east side of the present building.
3. This Shaker building was either the Deacon's House or the Boys' Shop.
4. Shaker Dwelling House, ca. 1834, now the manor house of Alasa Farms.
5. Old barn now housing Lake Plains Wildlife Rehabilitation Center.
6.-10. Large barns and other buildings; part of the working farm tour.

Planning Your Visit

Alasa Farms hosts the Sodus Shaker Festival in July on even-numbered years. It features lectures on Shaker life, craft demonstrations, Shaker music and dancing. Shaker reproductions are for sale. The Shaker Heritage Antique Show is held here annually in July, attracting many dealers in Shaker and Americana. Alasa Center offers various courses in arts and crafts, history, music, etc. during the first two weeks of August, annually. The first four weekends in October are Pick & Picnic weekends of apple picking. Tours of the working farm and the interior of the Shaker Dwelling House are available at these times, and also by appointment. Picnic benches available.

For further site /tour information contact:

Alasa Farms
Box 185
Alton, New York 14413.
Tel: 315/483-6321

For lodging/dining information contact:

The Greater Rochester Visitors Association
126 Andrews Street
Rochester, New York 14604
Tel: 716/546-3070

The Finger Lakes Association
309 Lake Street
Penn Yan, New York 14527
Tel: 800/548-4386

Access To Sodus

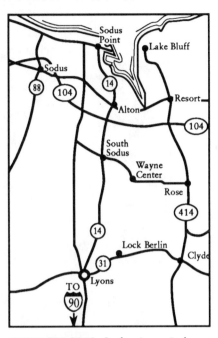

DIRECTIONS: Sodus is on Lake Ontario, about 15 miles north of Lyons, New York and 25 miles north of the New York State Thruway. Exit 42 from the Thruway and take Route 14 north to 104, then another 2 miles to Old Ridge Road. Continue straight across the intersection and you will be on Shaker Road. Alasa Farms is 1.8 miles north.

Admission
Fee

Limited
Handicapped
Access

Restrooms

Leashed
Pets Only

No
Credit Cards
Accepted

Verso of Groveland Fountain Stone

Inscription:

Written and placed here
On this chosen spot
By Divine Command

Engraved at New Lebanon

Erected Here May 18, 1843

Groveland 1843
I.N.Y.

GROVELAND

"Union Branch"
Sonyea, New York
1836-1892

Only Complete Fountain Stone
Tours & Special Events

In 1836 the Sodus Bay Shakers moved their community to the Town of Groveland ninety miles southwest of Sodus Bay. The Iroquois name for the new area was "Sonyea." The Shakers called the 1,800-acre site "Union Branch," a name which had originally belonged to the Shaker site at Gorham, Maine, by then closed. Its situation in Livingston County is one of the most beautiful areas of the Genesee River.

Today, only five of the more than thirty original Groveland buildings are left at the site. A sixth, the ca. 1839 East Family Office, has been moved to the Genesee Country Museum in Mumford. The Groveland Fountain Stone, the only complete one extant, is in the Livingston County Historical Society Museum in Geneseo.

History of the Site

Originally founded as a convenient stopping place between eastern and western Shaker villages, Groveland never became a large village, its highest number of Believers being about 125 in the years before the Civil War. Although it had excellent land and a nearby canal on which to ship its manufactures and agricultural products to market, there were not always enough hands to work, and the speed of railroads diminished the community's importance as a waystation for Shakers traveling from east to west.

East Meets Midwest

Groveland's architecture and manufactures—especially its distinctive "un-Shakerlike" furniture—markedly showed the

THE WORD OF THE LORD

Harken, oh ye children of men, to this the word of the Lord your God; yea, read, understand and give heed to the same. For with the finger of my own hand have I written it, and at my word was it engraved on this stone, which I have caused to be erected here, and called by the name,

The Lord's Stone

Thus saith Jehovah, Behold here have I opened a living fountain of holy and eternal waters, for the healing of the nations. Here have I chosen a sacred spot and commanded my people to consecrate and sanctify it unto me their Holy God. Here shall my name be owned, feared and praised; and I alone will be adored by the nations of the earth; and

unborn millions that shall pass this way shall bow in reverence to this, the work of my hands, saith the holy one of Israel, the Great I AM, the Almighty Power. Therefore, work with sacred reverence, and pass by in the solemn fear of his God, and let none presume to trifle with this my work, of his God, lest in my fierce anger for whosoever shall step upon this my holy ground, or lay their hands on this stone with an intent to do evil, or to injure it in any way, shall he no wise escape the justice of my righteous power. And in my own time will I, even I, bring an awful curse upon them, saith the Eternal Judge of all, and the Overruling Power of Heaven and earth.

Whose word is the truth. — Amen

Inscription on the Groveland Fountain Stone, engraved by Isaac Youngs.

influence of styles from both the East and Midwest. Groveland furniture did not have the light elegance typical of "classical" Shaker, but is described by writer Fran Kramer in her 1991 book as being "far from simple." Its best-known work was mainly created by Elder Emmory Brooks. Some Groveland furniture is described as large, with "curved skirts, turned knobs, paneled sides, and bulbous proportions," according to Mrs. Kramer. Much of Elder Emmory's work is made from black walnut, which grew at the site.

Groveland's architecture, too, was distinctive, showing a Victorian influence, including an Italianate design to the East Family Dwelling House, ca. 1859. This building was unequaled in the Genesee River valley. It had a hipped roof, stone pilasters, and a cupola that offered a view of the surrounding countryside.

Groveland survived until 1892, when most of its remaining thirty-four brothers and sisters moved to Watervliet, which unlike the heavily indebted Groveland was quite prosperous.

The State of New York brought the site from the Shakers, judging it an ideal facility for accommodating the 1,000-2,000 patients of the Craig Colony for Epileptics.

The state upgraded and modernized buildings, and also had the site landscaped by the famous firm of Olmstead Brothers of Brookline, Massachusetts. As time passed, however, buildings were lost to fire and old age, new ones were erected for the institution, and the Shaker legacy began to vanish. Craig Colony, itself, was doomed as New York State changed its policies for care of the handicapped from large institutional residences to small, group homes.

By the late 1980s, the Groveland site came into the hands of the expanding State prison system. The Rochester Area Shaker Study Group tried unsuccessfully to keep the Shaker buildings out of the prison complex, but three structures from the East Family were incorporated into the Groveland Correctional Institution. The former East Family Dwelling became the security headquarters, and its detached Kitchen and Sisters' Shop became places for inmates to meet visitors. These all can be seen from the

FRUIT HOUSE AND LAUNDRY.

THE SEWING HOUSE.

THE HOME OF THE SOCIETY OF CHRISTIAN BELIEVERS
VULGARLY CALLED SHAKERS.   SONYEA, LIVINGSTON, Co, N.Y.

1 OFFICE
2 HORSE BARN
3 MEETING HOUSE
4 DWELLING HOUSE
5 SEWING HOUSE
6 DINING ROOM & DAIRY

7 FRUIT HOUSE & LAUNDRY
8 STOCK BARN
9 WOOD & CARRIAGE HOUSE
10 BOILER HOUSE
11 JOINER SHOP
12 BROOM SHOP
13 SCHOOL HOUSE

Groveland in the late 19th century. Private collection.

prison parking lot. (The Dwelling was damaged by a lightning strike that caused a fire, destroying its distinctive cupola and all exterior architectural embellishments.)

The ca. 1839 Shaker Office building was moved to Mumford, New York, to be incorporated into a 19th-century village that is part of the Genesee Country Museum complex. In 1987, after prompting from the Rochester Area Shaker Study Group, the state installed a road sign and a site sign giving some information about the Shakers at Groveland.

Other Shaker artifacts are in the New York State Museum in Albany and in the Livingston County Historical Society Museum, Geneseo. One of the most important of these is the Fountain Stone from Groveland, which is housed in the Livingston County Museum. Erected at the center of a site of outdoor worship for Groveland Shakers in 1843, this is the only complete Fountain Stone remaining from all of Shakerdom. When the Shakers closed down their outdoor sites in the mid-19th century, all the Fountain Stones were destroyed or hidden to prevent them being desecrated by vandals. Only the Groveland stone remains fully intact.

Courtesy Livingston County Historical Society

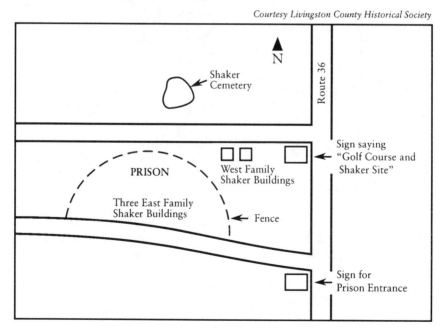

Planning Your Visit

While the three Groveland Shaker buildings within the prison are not open to the public, two West Family buildings outside the prison walls—the Sisters' Shop and the Office—can be seen from off State Route 36, just north of the prison. They are at the rear of the prison complex, down a paved road that also has sign posts for a nearby golf course. A water tower on a hill outside the prison helps mark the location of the adjacent Shaker cemetery, which is also on the hill.

The West Family Sisters' Shop has a small museum, operated by the Rochester Area Shaker Study Group. To visit the Sisters' Shop and Museum, permission must be obtained from the prison superintendent through the Shaker Study Group. The Cemetery can be viewed with no advance permission needed.

Family Trustees' Office building from Groveland. Other historic structures include an octagon house, a blacksmith and tinsmith shop, and a pioneer farmstead.

There are trade and craft demonstrations by costumed "villagers," as well as a gallery of sporting art, and a carriage museum; also gift shops and restaurants, including a garden pavilion.

Hours: The Genesee Country Museum is every day, 10 a.m.- 5 p.m. in July & August; closed on Monday May through June and September through October, open 10 a.m.-4 p.m.

| Admission Fee | Limited Handicapped Access | Restrooms | No Pets |

Major Credit Cards Accepted   Dining

Tourist Information

Genesee Country Museum
This reconstructed 19th-century village in a rural-garden setting has more than fifty town and farm buildings from western New York, including the ca. 1839 Shaker East

Livingston County Historical Society Museum
Operated by the Livingston County Historical Society. Besides Groveland Fountain Stone, collections include other Shaker items, Indian artifacts from the area, and Genesee Valley Heritage Collection. Also, the Wadsworth family memorabilia and nearby, the Wadsworth estates, two original family homes of this pioneer family, furnished with heirlooms.

The museum building is an old school built of cobblestone, a unique building method found in this area. There is a small gift shop.

Hours: The Livingston County Historical Society Museum is open Thursday and Sunday May through October 2 p.m.-5 p.m., or by appointment.

| Admission Fee | Limited Handicapped Access | Restrooms | No Pets |

Major Credit Cards Accepted

For further site/tour information contact:

Rochester Area Shaker Study Group
(To be put in touch with this group contact:)
Alasa Farms
Box 185
Alton, New York 14413

Livingston County Historical Society Museum
30 Center Street
Geneseo, New York 14454
Tel: 716/243-9147

Genesee Country Museum
PO Box 310
Flint Hill Road
Mumford, New York 14511
Tel: 716/538-6822

For lodging/dining information contact:

The Greater Rochester Visitors Association
126 Andrews Street
Rochester, New York 14604
Tel: 716/546-3070

The Finger Lakes Association
309 Lake Street
Penn Yan, New York 14527
Tel: 800/548-4386

Access to Groveland

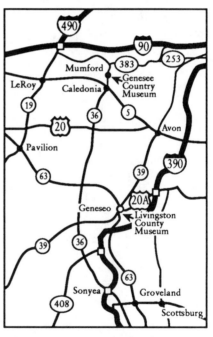

DIRECTIONS: Groveland ("Sonyea," the Shaker Site) is on Route 36 in Livingston County, about 40 miles due south of Rochester and 4 miles east of Exit 6 on I-390.

Take 390 south to the Sonyea

exit; go right (Route 36), about
2 miles. Follow the prison signs.

**For the Genesee Country
Museum:** coming from the east,
take exit 46 off the Thruway; 253
west; 383 south to Mumford; turn
right at yellow light on Flint Hill
Road. From the west, exit 47;
south on 19 to LeRoy; east on 5 to
Caledonia; north on 36 to Flint
Hill Road.

**To reach the Livingston County
Historical Society Museum:** take
390 South to the Geneseo exit.
Follow 20A southwest 6 miles to
Geneseo. Museum is at 30 Center
Street.

Shaker sisters of the North Union Centre Family dry skeins of yarn in the late 1800s.

NORTH UNION

"The Valley of God's Pleasure"
Shaker Heights, Ohio
1822-1889

Museum & Library
Self-Guided Tour & Special Programs

This site is now occupied by the modern residences of Shaker Heights. A self-guided walking tour of the area has been developed by the Shaker Historical Society, whose Museum houses a collection of Shaker furniture and other artifacts.

History of the Site

The North Union community, formed near the frontier town of Cleveland in 1822, was one of the last Shaker villages to be established. By 1850, when the number of Believers was at its peak nationally, North Union had about 300 residents, with buildings, three mills, and a school.

By 1889, the numbers had dwindled so that the community was closed and the remaining residents had moved to Watervliet, Ohio. In 1905, the property was sold to Cleveland entrepreneurs Oris P. and Mantis J. Van Sweringen, who developed "Shaker Village," now called the City of Shaker Heights, as one of the first "garden city" suburbs in the United States.

Today the legacy of the Shakers can be seen in the upper and lower "Shaker" lakes formed when the Shakers dammed

The massive 1843 grist mill built by the North Union Shakers was four stories high and said to be the finest of its day in Ohio. Eventually sold, it was blown up on July 4, 1886, by its owner. Illustration by A. M. Willard, mid-1800s.

Doan Brook to generate water power for their three mills. Shaker James Prescott, a stonemason by trade, laid the stone wall to dam the brook. He also wrote a detailed account of activities at North Union.

In the process of development—the building of fine homes, planting of trees, allocating of land for schools and houses of worship, and the establishing of a rapid-transit rail system to provide access to downtown Cleveland—all the original Shaker buildings were razed.

In 1947 the Shaker Historical Society was established, eventually opening a Museum in 1956 and in 1969 locating the Museum in a house coincidentally built on the site of the largest of the three North Union dwellings. Its foundation stones are thought to come from the grist mill blown up in 1886 as part of the Independence Day celebration.

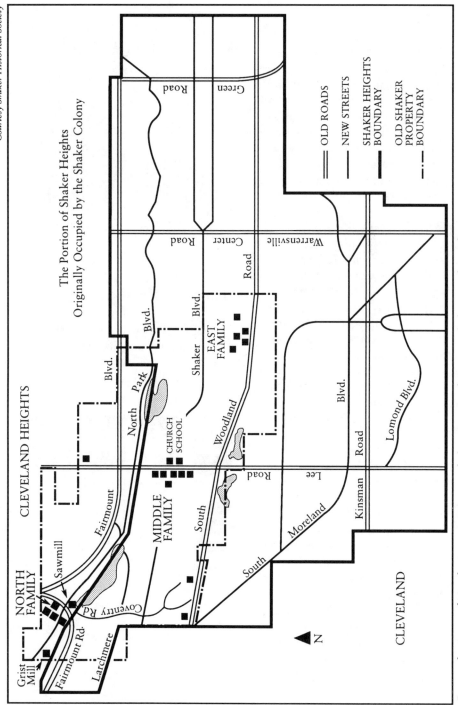

Courtesy Shaker Historical Society

The Portion of Shaker Heights
Originally Occupied by the Shaker Colony

OLD ROADS
NEW STREETS
SHAKER HEIGHTS BOUNDARY
OLD SHAKER PROPERTY BOUNDARY

CLEVELAND HEIGHTS

NORTH FAMILY

MIDDLE FAMILY

EAST FAMILY

CHURCH SCHOOL

Grist Mill

Sawmill

CLEVELAND

N

Green Road

Center Road

Warrensville

Shaker Blvd.

North Park Blvd.

Blvd.

Fairmount

Woodland Road

Lee Road

Kinsman Road

Moreland

South

Lomond Blvd.

Blvd.

Coventry Rd.

Fairmount Rd.

Larchmere

South

Former location of North Union. Courtesy Shaker Historical Society, Shaker Heights, Ohio.

Planning Your Visit

The Shaker Historical Museum houses a fine collection of Shaker furniture and artifacts from North Union and other Shaker sites and also has a library on its second floor containing an extensive holding of books, manuscripts, and archival materials. The library is open to members and also to researchers by appointment.

SPECIAL PROGRAMS

The Women's Committee provides volunteer support services to the Historical Society and sponsors the annual sale on the Museum grounds. It also presents special programs throughout the year, including lectures on Shaker and local history.

A wide variety of society-sponsored events and programs include changing historical exhibits, Museum open-houses for the public and for members only, guided tours for school groups, and lectures on the history and culture of the region.

Among the annual events are a benefit "Sale on the Grounds," a silent auction, and a summer "Shaker Social"; each autumn there is an "AppleFest" with apple products for sale, games, and craft demonstrations.

There is a quarterly newsletter, *The Journal,* and the museum has a shop, The Spirit Tree, with miniatures, reproductions, and gift items.

Courtesy Shaker Historical Society

Remains of the North Union grist mill at the turn of the century.

Tourist Information

Hours: Open year-round, Tuesday through Friday and Sunday 2-5 p.m. Closed holidays. Call or write to arrange special tours.

Donation Accepted

Limited Handicapped Access

Restrooms

No Pets

No Credit Cards Accepted

For further site/tour information contact:

The Shaker Historical Society
16740 South Park Boulevard
Shaker Heights, Ohio 44120
Tel: 216/921-1201

For lodging/dining information contact:

Convention & Visitors Bureau of Greater Cleveland
3100 Terminal Tower
Tower City Center
Cleveland, Ohio 44113
Tel: 800/321-1001 or
216/621-4110

Access to North Union

DIRECTIONS: Shaker Heights is in the greater Cleveland metropolitan area. From I-271: if coming from the north, take the Cedar Road exit; if coming from the south, take the Chagrin Boulevard exit. Go west to Richmond Road, turn (right if from south, left if from north) onto Shaker Boulevard and head west to Lee Road; turn right onto South Park Boulevard, then turn right to Shaker Historical Museum, fourth driveway on the right.

*Shakers standing near Marble Hall
around the turn of the century.*

UNION VILLAGE

"Wisdom's Paradise"
Lebanon, Ohio
1805-1912

Museums & Shops
Special Programs & Guided Tours
Gift Shops, Dining & Lodging

The remaining structures of the approximately sixty that once made up Union Village are two residences and a dairy wing that are part of the Otterbein United Methodist retirement homes. A fledgling Shaker museum in Marble Hall here has been operating since 1987. Most of the former Union Village's artifacts that belong to Otterbein are on loan to the Warren County Historical Society Museum nearby. Also in Lebanon is the Golden Lamb, an historic inn which houses a Shaker collection.

History of the Site

In the year 1805, three Shaker missionaries from Mount Lebanon proselytized in southwestern Ohio and found fertile soil. They were well met by New Light Presbyterians who were reacting against the Calvinism of their regional synod and attracted by the Shaker message.

Soon after arriving in the area, the missionaries had their first converts, at a place called Turtle Creek, in Warren County. The community known as Union Village was established there in 1805. Laying the foundation for a community patterned after Mount Lebanon, the Shaker missionaries lived in a log cabin while the land was cleared, roots and stumps dug up laboriously.

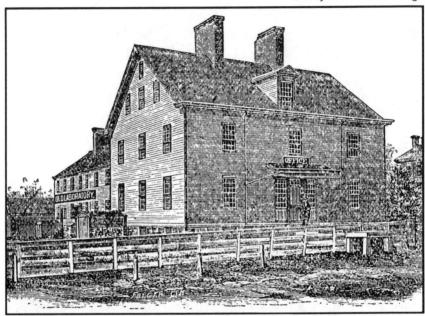

The Trustees' Office at Union Village in Lebanon, Ohio before its
1890s remodeling into Marble Hall. From Otterbein Homes Magazine.

The Elders' House was finished in 1807, a Meetinghouse
in 1810. It was a solid beginning, ultimately followed by
unsuccessful attempts to convert the local Indians, who still
posed a threat to the fragile white communities. Trouble also
came from border ruffians and enemies of the sect, who often
vandalized Shaker buildings, burning down their barn and
other buildings.

The Shakers persevered and by 1824 there were four
Shaker communities in Ohio: three in the southwest—
Watervliet (1806), Union Village (1805), and White Water
(1824)—and North Union, founded near Cleveland in 1822.
The most important was Union Village, the permanent residence of those missionaries who brought the gospel and
their authority into the region from Mount Lebanon. It
became the administrative and spiritual center, where the
elder and eldress were leaders of all the communities west of
the Appalachian Mountains.

Both former Shaker buildings here—the other is Bethany Hall, with thirty-two apartments—have been modernized, but the spectacular Victorian Marble Hall is close to its original state, with one of its Shaker-made cisterns for running water still intact.

When this typically modest 1810 Shaker Office was "improved" at great cost in the 1890s, many Believers were upset with the comparatively vainglorious design: turreted, with an ornamented cupola, a columned porch, marble floors, walnut paneling and a fancy staircase. Ironically, in recent years, attempts to have Marble Hall designated an historic site have been rebuffed on the grounds that the building's Victorian design is not Shaker!

With more than 4,000 acres of beautiful grounds, orchards, and farmland, this site is ideal for a retirement residence. It was sold in 1912 to a religious group which later merged with another to become the United Methodist Church. It was used as a home for children, and as a retirement residence, the Otterbein Homes. Under the terms of the 1912 sale, it was not until 1920 that the last of the Union Village Shakers left the site and moved to Canterbury.

Courtesy Otterbein Homes

The Trustees' Office after its remodeling.

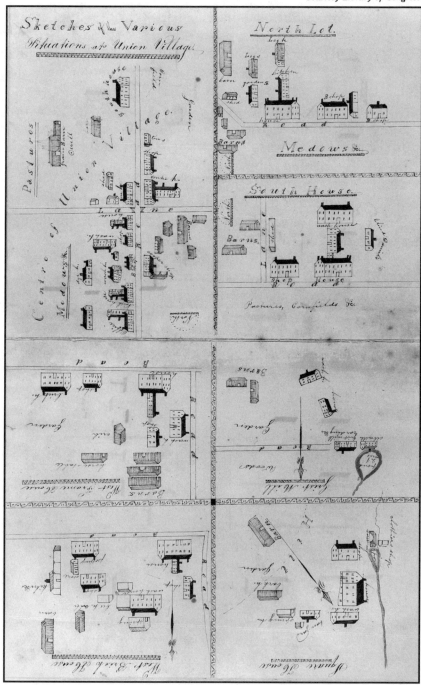

1835 map of Union Village by George Kendall after Isaac Youngs (1834).

Planning Your Visit

Otterbein Homes
Under the auspices of the Otterbein Archives Office, a museum is maintained on the ground floor of Marble Hall, the 1810 Shaker Trustees' Office, so named because of its marble-slab floor. The museum also displays a mix of antiques and artifacts in a large attic space.

A first-floor room has been dedicated to Shaker, and elsewhere on display are artifacts from the churches owning the structures.

Tourist Information

Tours are arranged through the Archives Office.

Hours: Otterbein Homes Office hours are 8 a.m.-4:30 p.m. daily.

No Admission Fee   Limited Handicapped Access   Restrooms   No Pets

The Warren County Historical Society Museum
This historical museum, in a community that is proud of having been established before Ohio became a state, has a range of exhibits of early Americana. These include a replicated pioneer cabin interior, a collection of horsedrawn vehicles, early farm tools, furniture and folk art, and a genealogy library.

Planning Your Visit

The museum's Shaker collection is displayed in the second-floor Robert and Virginia Jones Gallery. Most of the collection—one of the finest in the Midwest and one of the largest in the country—comes from Union Village and includes original manuscripts and ephemera. The museum shop offers Shaker reproductions, decorative accessories, and books.

SPECIAL PROGRAMS
The Warren County Historical Society offers year-round educational programming; write or call for a calendar of events.

Tourist Information

Museum Hours: Open year-round, Tuesday through Saturday 9 a.m.-4 p.m.; Sunday noon-4 p.m. Closed Mondays and holidays.

Admission Fee   Limited Handicapped Access   Restrooms   No Pets

Major Credit Cards Accepted

The Golden Lamb

This historic Inn is a Shaker museum in itself. Here, visitors not only view exhibits of Shaker, but, as guests, use them for sitting, sleeping, eating, etc., just as the Believers would have wanted.

Established in 1803, The Golden Lamb is now housed in a four-story structure that was added onto a two-story 1815 Federal brick building. The Inn flourished during the days of stagecoaches, and numbers among its guests ten United States presidents, Mark Twain, Charles Dickens, and Henry Clay.

Planning Your Visit

The Inn houses an extensive collection of artifacts and furniture, some from the East but most from southwestern Ohio. Two Shaker-furnished rooms on the fourth floor are glassed-in for display, and visitors are encouraged to explore the various floors of the Inn and to look at the various Shaker (and other) antiques that are part of the everyday decor.

The Shaker Dining Room on the main floor has a display of small Shaker artifacts and is of special interest to most guests. Artifacts and furniture may be inspected by qualified specialists and scholars with a prior appointment, and photography is permitted. There is no admission fee to tour the display rooms.

There are eighteen guest rooms, furnished with antiques as well as with telephone, air conditioning, private bath, and television. The Lamb Shop carries an array of gift items.

Tourist Information

Hours: The restaurant is open daily, except Christmas Day; lunch is served Monday through Sunday 11 a.m.-3 p.m.; dinner is served Monday through Thursday 5-9 p.m., Friday and Saturday 5-10 p.m., and Sunday 5-8 p.m. Reservations are accepted for all meals. The Inn serves a wide variety of midwest favorites in addition to seafood entrees.

The Lamb Shop is open Monday through Thursday 10:30 a.m.-9:30 p.m.; Friday and Saturday 10:30 a.m.-10:30 p.m.; Sunday 10:30 a.m.-8:30 p.m.

No Admission Fee   Limited Handicapped Access   Restrooms   No Pets

Major Credit Cards Accepted   Dining   Lodging

For further site /tour information contact:

**Otterbein Homes
Archives Office**
585 North State Route 741
Lebanon, Ohio 45036
Tel: 513/932-2020

**Warren County Historical
Society Museum**
105 South Broadway
PO Box 223
Lebanon, Ohio 45036
Tel: 513/932-1817

The Golden Lamb
27 South Broadway
Lebanon, Ohio 45036
Tel: 513/932-5065

For additional lodging/dining information contact:

**Warren County Convention
& Visitors Bureau**
777 Columbus Avenue
Lebanon, Ohio 45036
Tel: 513/933-1138

Access to Union Village

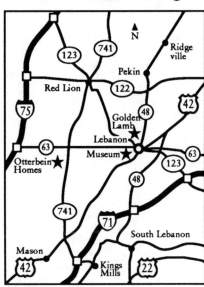

DIRECTIONS: Lebanon is approximately 30 miles north of Cincinnati and 24 miles south of Dayton. The Otterbein Homes are 5 miles southwest of Lebanon on State Route 63 at 741. For the Warren County Historical Society Museum: from I-75 go east on Route 63 to South Broadway. Turn right and the Museum is on the right; from I-71 go west on Main Street (State Route 123) and turn left on Broadway. The Museum is on the right. The Golden Lamb is at 27 South Broadway (at the junction of Routes 48 and 63), just north of the Warren County Historical Society Museum.

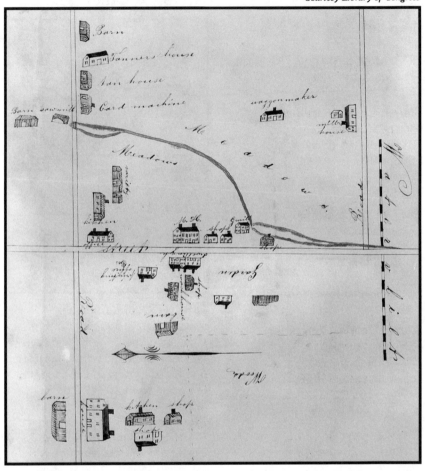

Barn
Tanners house
tan house
Card machine
Barn sawmill
waggonmaker
Meadow
Meadows
kitchen
H. H.
shop
Smith
Shop
Street
Garden
Meadow
barn
kitchen shop
shop

1835 Map of Watervliet settlement by George Kendall, after Isaac Youngs (1834).

WATERVLIET

"Vale of Peace"
Dayton, Ohio
1806-1900

Museum & Shop
Guided & Self-guided Tour, Special Programs

Watervliet Shaker Village was located in what is now Dayton (in the language of midwestern survey maps: in Section 13, 14 and 17, Township 2, Range 7 in Van Buren Township, Montgomery County, Ohio). Most of the site today is a commercial development of 1980s office buildings, the Miami Valley Research Park. No Shaker buildings remain. The rest of the site, an adjacent farm in Greene County, is now Bugamo Center, used for Catholic retreats. A marker erected by the Kettering-Moraine Museum marks the approximate site of the Shaker Cemetery.

The Kettering-Moraine Museum and Historical Society is a complex of six historic buildings (ranging from 1803-1890), plus the main exhibition building, on the southern edge of the City of Kettering. The Museum was founded in 1962 to preserve artifacts from the region.

Two structures have survived from Watervliet and been moved to the museum. One, reassembled and open to the public, is the ca. 1819 Miller's House, originally located on Patterson Road within the Shaker Community. The second Watervliet building, the Tannery Barn, used there as the stable, is still dismantled and awaits reconstruction when funds are available.

History of the Site

This Village was "gathered" at Beulah, near Dayton, in 1806. It was called Watervliet, in honor of Mother Ann's first home in upstate New York.

The Isaac Youngs map of Watervliet Village in July 1834 shows as many as twenty-nine structures on its 800 acres. (Of these, 700 were in Montgomery County. The remaining 100 were over the county line in Greene County.) By then there were four families living here. There was a Meetinghouse, Office and a large Dwelling at the site. The Village at its height had about 100 members, and a Gristmill, Sawmill, and wool-carding machine, as well as a Wagon-making Shop, Printing Office, and a Tannery.

Courtesy of Kettering-Moraine Museum

The ca. 1819 Shaker Miller's House from Watervliet, Ohio.

Interior of Shaker Miller's House from Watervliet, Ohio.

A significant aspect of Watervliet was that one of the most influential Shaker writers and theologians lived here. Richard McNemar moved to Watervliet in 1832, and under his religious name, "Eleazar Wright," wrote and published religious, philosophical, and historical tracts. These were printed here and distributed throughout Shakerdom.

Regional Furniture Style

Watervliet Shakers, as with other Ohio Shakers, were known for their furniture-making and developed a regional style unlike that of the eastern Shaker furniture makers. Their craftsmen were more interested than traditional Shaker craftsmen in the decoration of their pieces, and Ohio Shaker chairs may have distinctive coloration.

Planning Your Visit

The Kettering-Moraine Museum sits on 3.5 acres, with the various historic buildings sited in a circular cluster. The ca. 1819 Miller's House from Watervliet is here. (The miller, wagon-maker, and possibly the blacksmith lived in this house.) Among other relocated structures here are two very early 19th-century log cabins, an 1841 Greek Revival house, and the 1817 pioneer house of Peter Hetzel.

A single Shaker bed originates from Mount Lebanon, New York, and dates from early 1800. The homespun wool blanket is from Pleasant Hill, Kentucky, and beside the bed is a washstand from Watervliet.

A number of artifacts from Watervliet are on exhibit, and for sale in the gift shop are reproductions such as oval boxes and books on Shaker. A local history book about Bertha Furey, *Summers at Watervliet* by Melba Hunt, is available here.

Also in the Museum's general collection are artifacts from Dayton's own inventors, the Wright brothers, as well as historic items from the early days of the automobile. The buildings also include the former Kettering Court House, which is now the main exhibition hall.

Tourist Information

Group tours of the Museum are given during the week by appointment. Lectures and special seasonal programs are given regularly. Call or write for schedule.
Museum hours: Sundays, 1-5 p.m.

Admission Fee — Limited Handicapped Access — Restrooms — No Pets

No Credit Cards Accepted

For further site/tour information contact:

Kettering-Moraine Museum and Historical Society
35 Moraine Circle South
Kettering, Ohio 45439-1927
Tel: 513/299-2722

For lodging/restaurant information contact:

Dayton-Montgomery County Convention & Visitors Bureau
Chamber Plaza
5th & Main Streets
Dayton, Ohio 45402-2400
Tel: 513/226-2400

Access to Watervliet

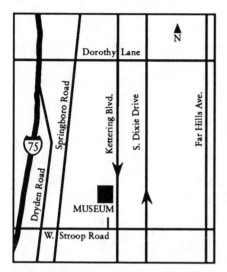

DIRECTIONS: From I-75 North, take Exit 50B, Springboro Road, and follow West Stroop Road eastward to Moraine Circle South. From I-75 South, take Exit 47, Kettering-Moraine, and follow Dorothy Lane eastward to Kettering Boulevard; turn right, and Museum is on the right.

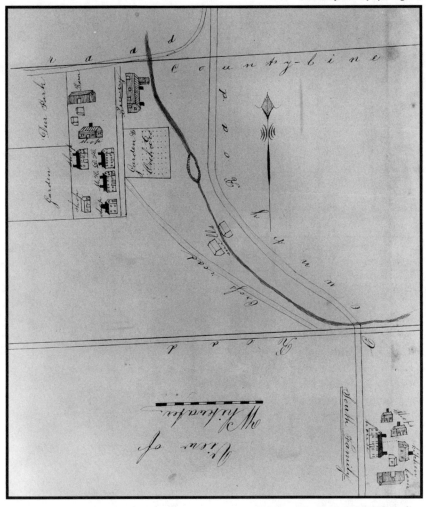

*Isaac Youngs' 1834 Map of
White Water, Ohio settlement.*

WHITE WATER

"Lonely Plain of Tribulation"
Hamilton County, Ohio
1822-1916

There are twenty-three established or suspected Shaker structures remaining of this Village, founded by the Shakers on the banks of the dry fork of the White Water River ca. 1822. The buildings all are under the management of the Hamilton County Park District and the entire site is currently closed to the public.

There are extensive, long-term plans for future restoration of the site, but at present the buildings are occupied by tenants. Research about White Water is ongoing, and the Park District has worked steadily at acquiring and protecting the site and surrounding land.

History of the Site

White Water was not successful at first, due to much illness from cholera epidemics. That and the poor soil of the first land they farmed combined to make the settlement dependent on other Shaker communities for aid. As they expanded to better land they improved their situation, and when it was finally sold in 1916 White Water had survived longer than the other Ohio Shaker villages. (It is still some of the most productive farmland in the state.)

A Shaker Brother standing by the Meetinghouse at White Water around the turn of the century. From the collection of the Shaker Museum and Library, Old Chatham, New York.

In 1827, White Water was enlarged by an influx of Believers who abandoned their failed settlement at West Union, Indiana (Busro). The Village grew to number 175 persons in three families, who are thought to have lived and worked in as many as sixty buildings on 1,200 acres.

Little is known about daily activities at White Water because most of the archives and papers were destroyed when the Centre Family Dwelling burned down in 1907.

There were a grist mill, sawmill, and a broom-making shop, several barns, a brewery where malt beer was made for sale, as well as workshops, a grainery, and sheds.

In 1916, the Shakers sold the land as three farms, and the land remained with the new owners until 1974, when the North Family farm was sold. A portion of this became a housing development. During 1989-1991, the Park District acquired the South and Centre Family acreage and the remaining undeveloped portion of the North Family farm. Acquisition of the land was in fulfillment of a pledge to local citizens to preserve additional natural resources if the voters passed a 1988 park levy.

The White Water site is unique among Shaker Villages in that its Meetinghouse was located at the North Family. Because the Shakers expanded their land holdings and moved southward, the original Centre Family became the North Family. However, a Meetinghouse was never constructed at the new Centre Family and the Shakers continued using the one at the North Family.

The Meetinghouse, North Family Dwelling, and Centre Family Office and Shop are brick; the rest are frame. There are also a number of 20th-century sheds, coops, etc., which are not Shaker-built.

The remaining buildings, from the South, Centre and North families, include: the 1827 Meetinghouse; the Centre Family Trustees' Office, 1855; the North Family Dwelling, 1832, and Seed Shop, ca. 1856; the South Family Dwelling (not built by Shakers), 1840; the Milk/Loom House, 1855; the 1876 Broom Shop; the 1853 Blacksmith Shop (which had other uses as well); the 1875 Grain Barn; and the 1849 Milk house.

In the Cemetery, more than 100 Believers are buried.

Planning Your Visit

No site or historic markers are in place at the site, and there is no off-road parking. The Hamilton County Park District administration prohibits individual visitors to the area, which is wholly within its boundaries. Group tours are sometimes arranged by the Park District, for groups with a special interest focus, such as Shakers or historic preservation.

For further site/tour information contact:

Hamilton County Park District
Administrative Office
10245 Winton Road
Cincinnati, Ohio 45231
Tel: 513/521-PARK

For lodging/dining information contact:

Greater Cincinnati Convention and Visitors Bureau
300 West Sixth Street
Cincinnati, Ohio 45202
Tel: 513/621-6994

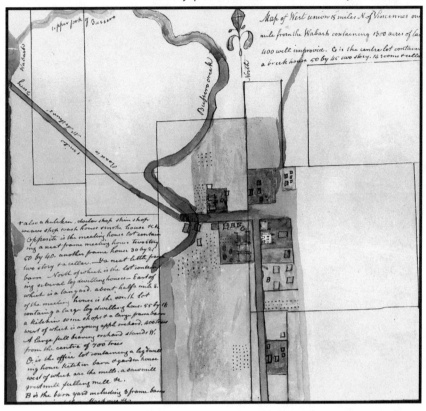

*Shaker Village of West Union, Indiana.
Attributed to Richard McNemar,
ca. 1824-1827.*

"Map of West Union 15 miles N. of Vincennes one mile from the Wabash containing 1,300 acres of land 400 well improved. C is the centre lot containing a brick house 50 by 45 two story. 14 Rooms and cellar and also kitchen, doctor shop, skin shop, weave shop, wash house smoke house. Opposite is the meetinghouse lot containing a great frame meetinghouse two story 50 by 40. Another frame house 30 by 21 two story and a cellar—a neat little frame barn North of which is the lot containing several log dwelling houses—East of which is a barnyard, about half a mile S. of the meetinghouse is the south lot containing a large log dwelling house 55 by 18 a kitchen some shops and a large frame barn west of which is a young apple orchard, 400 trees. A large full bearing orchard stands W. from the centre of 700 trees O is the office lot containing a log dwelling house kitchen barn and garden house west of which are the mills. A sawmill grist mill fulling mill. B is the barnyard including 3 frame barns threshing and flax machines."

WEST UNION

No Spiritual Name
Knox County, Indiana
1807-1827

Archaeological Dig Ongoing

This westernmost outpost of Shakerdom also known as Busro, was established in 1807 and lasted until 1827. At its peak, there were 300 members at West Union, and it was as dynamic and promising as Pleasant Hill and South Union in Kentucky. There are only archaeological remains at the site, which is now a residential and farming area.

History of the Site

Situated in Knox County, upon rich Wabash River bottomland and within reach of the Mississippi and Ohio water highways, Busro had many advantages as a settlement. Its most serious disadvantage, however, was the malaria that sickened many Believers and ultimately contributed to the closing of the Village.

The first, and temporary, breakup of Busro occurred during the War of 1812, when Indian hostilities erupted along the western frontier and there was the threat of British invasion from Canada. The Shaker Village was sixteen miles north of strategic Fort Knox, on a traditional path of Indian attacks. During the war, there were other difficulties than danger from the Indians, however, as earthquakes in 1811-1812 sent the rivers running upstream.

Finally, with the nearby quartering of 1,400 rowdy militiamen, the Shakers decided West Union had to be temporarily abandoned by its 300 Believers, with their stock and baggage.

Return to Try Again

The war almost over, the Shakers returned to Busro in 1814. Malarial sickness continued, however, and there were also bitter factional dissension and disagreements among the members, causing internal turmoil. These problems persisted.

By 1826, regular visits by Shaker leaders from other communities still had been ineffectual in resolving the difficulties. By the spring of 1827, the approximately 100 Shakers remaining at Busro departed wholesale by boat, wagon, and foot, dispersing to settle at Pleasant Hill and South Union, Kentucky, and White Water and other Ohio communities.

Closing Busro, according to historian Stephen J. Stein, "represented a major defeat for the United Society's strategy of geographical expansion." Stein writes, "Although West Union was not the first site to be abandoned by the Shakers, it was the largest and most significant."

Through the decades, the Busro site has all but vanished, but local Shaker historians are working to determine what was there and what remains.

Auburn, Indiana, historian John Martin Smith has located the site through contemporary land records. Subsequently, archaeological probes conducted under the sponsorship of the Indiana Historical Society confirmed the existence of foundations and artifacts at the site.

Courtesy John Martin Smith

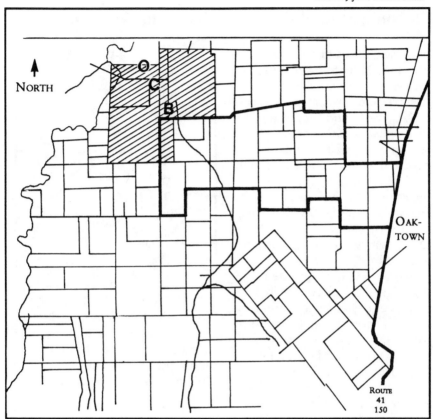

Site Map of Busro as it looks today. Shaker site is shaded on the map. Location of former Office Family, Centre Family, and Barnyard are indicated by letters. To reach the site turn left at main intersection in Oaktown. Continue west and north (right). Local roads here have no names, so turn carefully. If you go west to the creek, the mill was located south of the present iron bridge. In low water you can see a large wooden beam from the mill along the east side of the creek bank.

Planning Your Visit

Nothing remains of the Shaker buildings. Refer to the old map at the beginning of the chapter and the present-day site map on page 207. C, the Centre Family, was on the southwest corner of the inter-section of the main northbound road and the road going west to the creek. The Meetinghouse was opposite. B, the Barnyard, was just south of the Centre Dwelling, etc., on the east side of the road. The Office Family was on the north above the Centre Family.

Most of the site is privately owned by the Cardinal family, which has been tolerant of persons seriously investigating Busro. Visitors to this site should respect the family's privacy and be careful not to damage crops in fields.

For further site information contact:

Indiana Historical Society
315 West Ohio Street
Indianapolis, Indiana 46202
Tel: 317/232-1882

John Martin Smith
PO Box 686
Auburn, Indiana 46706
Tel: 219/925-4560

For lodging/dining information contact:

Chamber of Commerce
27 North Third Street
PO Box 553
Vincennes, Indiana 47591

Access to West Union

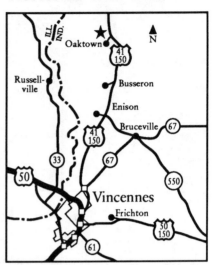

DIRECTIONS: Take Route 41 north from Vincennes to Oaktown. At main intersection, turn left, or turn left at the next intersection north. (Refer to site map on page 207 for enlarged view of area.)

Spiral staircase, 1839 Trustees' Office.
Built by Micajah Burnett. Courtesy
Shaker Village of Pleasant Hill.

PLEASANT HILL

No Known Spiritual Name
Harrodsburg, Kentucky
1805-1910

National Historic Landmark

Exhibit Rooms & Educational Programs

Gift & Craft Shop, Lodging & Dining

Tours, Riverboat Rides

Visitors to the restored Shaker village at Pleasant Hill find themselves in one of Kentucky's most beautiful settings, surrounded by 2,700 acres of bluegrass farmland. This was the first historic site in the United States to be designated a National Historic Landmark from boundary to boundary.

Known as Shakertown at Pleasant Hill, this restored community has thirty Shaker buildings and is, perhaps, the most varied and self-contained of all the Shaker sites.

Open year-round, it has more than 250,000 annual visitors who experience the "living history" of Shaker life in the midst of first-rate examples of Shaker architecture. With magnificent buildings and graceful details designed by Micajah Burnett, Pleasant Hill has a Midwestern look in keeping with Shaker standards of simplicity and functionalism.

History of the Site

Pleasant Hill was founded in 1805 by three Shakers who came westward on foot from Mount Lebanon, New York. They were sent to preach to the great camp meetings of a revivalist movement sweeping the frontier. By 1830, this

Photo: *James L. Ballard*

Micajah Burnett

A self-taught architect and engineer, Brother Micajah led in the development and building at Pleasant Hill and several other Midwestern Shaker communities. Courtesy Shaker Village of Pleasant Hill.

Centre Family Dwelling, designed by Burnett and completed in 1834 after ten years of construction, is made of limestone, known locally as "Kentucky marble."

thriving community of Believers in Mercer County was prospering, with more than 4,000 acres of farmland and woods in the midst of a bountiful country. Sometimes called Shawnee Creek for a stream close by, it had almost 500 inhabitants and was one of the largest Shaker villages.

In the mid-19th century the Shakers at Pleasant Hill led the state in scientific farming, including the propagation of sheep, cattle, and hogs and the development of farm implements. Like other Shaker communities, the Village became known for garden seeds, flatbrooms, and preserves. The Shakers also managed a busy landing on the nearby Kentucky River, which they used for trade out to the Ohio and Mississippi rivers. After Union Village, Ohio, Pleasant Hill was the second most important Shaker settlement in the Midwest.

The 1809 Farm Deacon's Shop was the first permanent structure within the Village.

In the Way of Armies

Already experiencing the decline in numbers common to many Shaker sites during this period, the Village suffered serious setbacks during the four-year tumult of the Civil War as troops from both the Union and Confederate armies marched through on campaigns and raids. Often, armed men of both sides forcibly impressed horses and wagons, hay and fodder from the Shakers, who were left with useless promissory notes for repayment. War-weary, ragged troops, invariably hungry and thirsty, sometimes surrounded the central well "like the locusts of Egypt" or begged for food at the windows and doors of the houses.

Early 20th-century portrait of Sister Mary Settles, the last Shaker of Pleasant Hill, with the Centre Family Dwelling behind.

By the end of the war, in 1865, Believers numbered 385. After the war, Pleasant Hill continued to decline, with 234 members in 1875. By 1910, they had diminished to only twelve. It was then that the property was sold.

Over the next fifty years individual buildings changed ownership a number of times. In 1961 a nonprofit organization was formed by private citizens to preserve the Village as a living museum and restore it to its appearance before the Civil War.

In 1968, with almost half the buildings under renovation or completed, the doors of the Museum were opened to the public. Restoration work is ongoing including the rerouting of U.S. 68 away from the Village.

Distinctive Architecture

The impressive "Shaker Georgian"-style brick buildings of Pleasant Hill were for the most part designed by Shaker architect Micajah Burnett, a native of Virginia. These include one of the finest examples of extant Shaker architecture: the Centre Family Dwelling, made of limestone known locally as Kentucky marble. Begun in 1824, the massive dwelling was finished ten years later. Divided for men and women, it housed 100 residents in more than forty rooms on a total of four stories.

One of the most notable features in the Village is found in the Trustees' Office, where twin spiral staircases rise magnificently through three floors, ending in a skylight. Begun in 1839, this building, too, is the work of Micajah Burnett, who as a self-taught architect and an accomplished civil engineer also directed the development of the public waterworks (the first west of the Allegheny Mountains) and later traveled to other Shaker villages to manage construction projects.

In general, Shaker architecture in Kentucky uses distinctive arches and also has higher ceilings (because of the warmer climate) than do the buildings of the East.

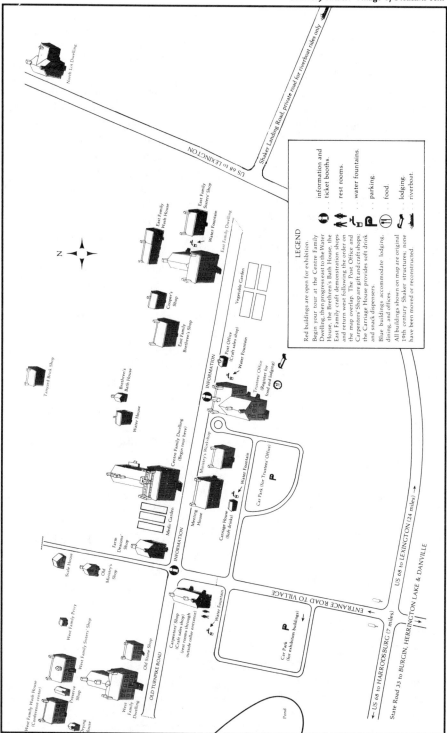

Site Map of Pleasant Hill today.

Planning Your Visit

Collections of Shaker furniture and artifacts are on display in six of the eleven exhibition buildings. The over thirty restored buildings include: the ca. 1824 Centre Family Dwelling, 1839 Trustees' Office, 1817 East Family Dwelling, 1820 Meetinghouse, 1821 West Family Dwelling, 1815 Carpenter's Shop, 1833 Water House, various Workshops and Wash Houses, The Post Office, Carriage House, Tannery, Drying House, Stable and a Privy.

There are also a vegetable garden and a garden for medicinal herbs known as the Medic Garden.

Walking tours of the Village are self-guided, with interpretive staff on hand to present and explain aspects of Shaker life and history. Allow at least two hours for the tour, but expect to stay longer to enjoy the site.

An admission fee is charged, but children five years of age and younger are free. Most events are included in the price of a Village tour ticket. Special one-price plans for overnight guests include meals, lodging, tour ticket, and special programs.

SPECIAL PROGRAMS

Living history programs at Pleasant Hill include the singing of Shaker songs by a Village interpreter (mid-March through November) and artisans in Shaker dress demonstrating crafts such as basketweaving, carpentry, chair-making, and textile skills. Cooking demonstrations, silk-culturing, and shearing of sheep are regularly performed.

A varied calendar of year-round special events includes music/dance performances, visiting artisans, the Celebration of Autumn in September, and Winter Weekends in January and February. Winter Weekends include lodging Friday and Saturday nights, five meals, admission to the Village and all activities as well as a special Shaker music program on Saturday.

Special weekend programs are scheduled throughout the year, including river excursions, wildflower hikes, Shaker worship services and a performance by the Louisville Ballet.

Gift and craft shops feature Shaker reproduction furniture and handmade items from Pleasant Hill as well as other handmade Kentucky articles.

Meeting facilities are also available, including meeting rooms and sitting rooms.

Riverboat trips are available several times daily, from late April through October, on the 150-passenger sternwheeler Dixie Belle, leaving from Shaker Landing and travelling for an hour along a scenic stretch of the Kentucky River known as the Palisades. There are other excursions and special programs available throughout the year. Combination rates with the Village tour and group rates are available. The boat can be chartered.

Tourist Information

Hours: Exhibition buildings are open year-round, daily, 9 a.m.-6 p.m. Hours and the number of buildings open vary from Thanksgiving weekend to mid-March. Gift Shop open year-round, daily, 9 a.m.-6 p.m.; winter hours are until 5 p.m.

Dining: The Trustees' Office dining room is open year-round, featuring Shaker-style entrees and Kentucky country fare. Times for seating in the dining room are available at the ticket booths or at the inn desk at the Trustees' Office. There is a no-tipping policy. Meals are served at several seatings: buffet breakfast, luncheon and dinner; children's menus are available.

Summer Kitchen: Additional midday dining, featuring a light menu, is available summer and fall in the West Family Dwelling cellar. Reservations are advisable.

Lodging: Located in fifteen original buildings throughout the Village, overnight rooms are available year-round and have air-conditioning, private baths, telephone, and television, with reproduction Shaker furniture and hand-woven rugs and curtains.

Rates vary according to room size and location; no charge for children seventeen and under when occupying room with parents. Reservations as far in advance as possible.

For further site/tour information contact:

Shakertown at Pleasant Hill
3500 Lexington Road
Harrodsburg, Kentucky 40330
Tel: 606/734-5411

For additional lodging/dining information contact:

Tourist Commission
103 South Main
PO Box 283
Harrodsburg, Kentucky 40330
Tel: 606/734-2364

Admission Fee	Limited Handicapped Access	Restrooms	No Pets

Major Credit Cards Accepted	Dining	Lodging

Access to Pleasant Hill

DIRECTIONS: Shakertown at Pleasant Hill is on U.S. Route 68, 25 miles southwest of Lexington and 7 miles northeast of Harrodsburg. The village is 24 miles from north-south I-75, 22 miles from east-west I-64, and 84 miles from north-south I-65.

*Believers pose (ca. 1885) near
the 1818 Meetinghouse; in the
background is the Centre Family
Dwelling, where the museum is
housed.*

SOUTH UNION

"Jasper Valley"
South Union, Kentucky
1807-1922

Last Shaker Post Office

Museum & Library

Educational Programming, Tours

Gift Shop, Lodging & Dining

Established in 1807 on 6,000 acres in south-central Kentucky, South Union was given the spiritual name "Jasper Valley." Only nine structures remain, but ongoing archaeological work has confirmed that at least 215 other buildings once stood on this site.

Four of the remaining buildings, well-preserved and surrounded by attractive gardens and lawns, belong to a nonprofit organization and are open to the public. In addition to the imposing 1824 Centre Family Dwelling, they include the 1869 Shaker Tavern, the 1917 Shaker Store and Post Office, and the recently restored ca. 1835 Smoke and Milk House. The other five surviving buildings are owned privately but can be seen from the road.

The four restored buildings open to visitors are managed by a preservation group known as Shakertown at South Union, Inc. This group operates the site, with its own newsletter (*The South Union Messenger*) as an important means of communication. They also hold fundraisers such as their annual gala.

A small library in the Centre House has a collection of old photographs, manuscripts, printed material, and ephem-

1824 Centre Family Dwelling hallway, showing double doors and stairways, one for males, one for females.

era, but most of the community's extensive manuscript collection is housed at the Kentucky Library on the campus of Western Kentucky University in Bowling Green, fifteen miles east of the South Union site.

The Post Office is on Highway 73, several miles from the Museum. The only still-operating former Shaker Post Office, it was established in 1826.

The Smoke and Milk House opened for visitors in mid-1992 after six years of restoration work. It has antique equipment for making butter and cheese as well as a collection of wooden dairy tools.

The privately owned South Union buildings include the massive 1854 brick Wash House, owned by the Fathers of Mercy, who also own the Steam House, built in 1847 for warming cattle feed. The Ministry Shop, built in 1846, is a private residence, and the ca. 1840 barn also is privately owned.

1869 Shaker Tavern, a hotel built by the South Union Believers for travelers.

History of the Site

Like Pleasant Hill in Harrodsburg, Kentucky, South Union found itself overrun by maneuvering armies during the Civil War. The Shakers were pacifists and as such were not much loved or protected by either side. In one period, more than 20,000 fence rails were torn down and burned by bivouacked federal troops. South Union was nearly driven into poverty, but the Village survived, although material losses during the war contributed to its decline. In 1912 South Union was compelled to begin closing down, its members having dwindled to fewer than forty from a peak of 400 in the 1820s.

In its heyday, South Union was famous for the quality of its stock and produce, and some of its crafts and foodstuffs earned a national reputation for excellence. Although some Shaker communities abstained from alcohol, South Union ran a whiskey distillery built in 1823.

Textile work, such as woven rugs and women's bonnets and kerchiefs made of silk from the community's own silkworms, was famous across the country. South Union sisters were known for their preserves, and their poultrymen raised first-quality chickens for wholesale. South Union and Pleasant Hill were both successfully selling seeds across the South and Midwest as far away as New Orleans.

Preserving the Legacy

By the turn of the century, buildings and workshops were no longer in use, members were aging, and hired hands had to be brought in to do much of the work—the same symptoms affecting other failing Shaker communities in the last decades of the 19th century. The nine surviving members of the South Union group had moved away by September 1922, when an investment company purchased the community.

The closing of South Union effectively brought an end to a hundred years of western Shakerism. The United Society of Believers no longer had a community west of the Appalachians.

With interest in the Shaker legacy growing through the 1960s, preservation efforts finally began to bear fruit in 1971, when Shakertown at South Union, Inc. purchased the first buildings.

Courtesy Shakertown at South Union, Museum Collection

1810 Dwelling, the first permanent structure at South Union.

Courtesy Shakertown at South Union

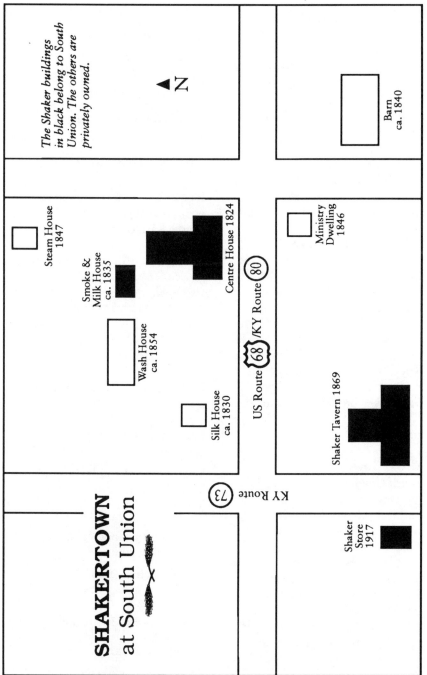

SHAKERTOWN at South Union

The Shaker buildings in black belong to South Union. The others are privately owned.

N

Steam House 1847

Smoke & Milk House ca. 1835

Wash House ca. 1854

Silk House ca. 1830

Centre House 1824

Barn ca. 1840

Ministry Dwelling 1846

US Route 68/KY Route 80

KY Route 73

Shaker Tavern 1869

Shaker Store 1917

Planning Your Visit

The visit begins at the Shaker Museum in the Centre Family Dwelling, the most prominent building in the community. Once home to ninety Shakers, the Centre House has forty-two rooms and is furnished with original Shaker artifacts. The Museum Shop in the Centre House offers Shaker reproductions, books, baskets, oval boxes, tinware, candles, and herbs.

SPECIAL PROGRAMS

The Museum offers a year-round calendar of events which include workshops, lectures, musical performances (there is a South Union Shaker Quartet), and various crafts demonstrations. Special events include the Fall Candlelight Tour, the South Union Seminar with speakers on Shaker, a November Shaker Breakfast, and the Christmas at Shakertown Celebration.

Shaker Tavern

South Union is on a busy highway midway between Bowling Green and Russellville, and the Shakers operated a thriving inn for more than thirty years, catering to railroad travelers for the most part. The Shaker Tavern has been put back in use as an inn and offers overnight bed & breakfast accommodations (six rooms). It also is open for lunch Tuesday through Saturday 11:30 a.m.- 2 p.m.

Shakertown
South Union

Tourist Information

Hours: The Shaker Museum is open Monday through Saturday, March 15-November 15, 9 a.m.-5 p.m. and on Sundays 1-5 p.m. The Museum Shop is open during Museum hours. The Museum is also open for tours November 15 through March 15, by appointment.

South Union Post Office is open year-round; Tel: 502/542-6757.

For lodging at the Shaker Tavern B&B: Tel: 502/542-6801

For further site/tour information contact:

Shakertown at South Union
South Union, Kentucky 42283
Tel: 502/542-4167

For additional lodging/dining information contact:

Tourist Commission
352 Three Springs Road
PO Box 1040
Bowling Green, Kentucky
42101-1040
Tel: 800/326-7465

Chamber of Commerce
Russellville, Kentucky 42276

Access to South Union

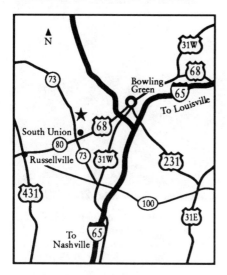

DIRECTIONS: Shakertown at South Union is 10 miles west of Bowling Green, 114 miles southwest of Louisville, and 60 miles north of Nashville.

From I-65 take Exit 20, Green River Parkway, to Exit 5, U.S. 68-80; turn left and follow the signs approximately 10 miles to South Union.

Admission Fee   Limited Handicapped Access   Restrooms   Pets Permitted Outside Only

Major Credit Cards Accepted   Dining   Lodging

*McKinnon House (left), 1894, was
used by Shakers and the ca. 1899
Dwelling (right, slightly behind),
was built by Shakers at White Oak.*

*"...the best people and neighbors; scrupulously honest
in all their dealings with their fellow man."*

*White Oak, Georgia neighbor
on the Shaker Colony*

WHITE OAK

No Spiritual Name
White Oak, Georgia
1898-1902

Last "Colony" Planted

Little remains of this brief but costly foray into the South by Ohio Shakers in 1898. Where once a modern new dwelling was erected and over 60,000 acres of magnificent plantation lay ready for development, there is only a memory. One building is left—a pre-existing structure now privately owned.

By 1898, Shakers were much more "of" the world than early Believers ever would have expected. Throughout the second half of the 19th century, leaders of the order had considerable cash at their disposal, especially after the sale of villages and land holdings. This cash often was invested in commercial paper, and at other times was used to purchase timberland for harvesting or to buy real estate on speculation.

In this time, the Shaker Order was considered a significant player in the world of finance. Understandably, not all ventures succeeded, one of the most glaring failures being the Georgia enterprise. The short-lived White Oak colony was undertaken by leading Union Village, Ohio, Shakers—ostensibly to find a climate where Believers could live more comfortably yet still prosper.

History of the Site

The Union Village leadership first purchased two pre-Civil War plantations totaling close to 10,000 acres for the bargain price of less than $30,000. Before the war, the Altama and Hopeton plantations were said to have been valued at $600,000, but by 1898 were in desperate need of rehabilitation. This the Shakers set out to do, reclaiming rice fields, repairing buildings, and shipping in livestock and goods from Ohio.

Soon, another 51,000 acres were acquired in Pierce, Charleton, and Ware Counties. Most of this tract was near Nahunta, an area that later became part of Brantley County. This property was never developed.

The Altama plantation in Glynn County is where the Shakers first lived, in a large existing house, before moving to the Hopeton plantation at White Oak in Camden County, where there was a fine, almost new residence. In addition, hired help there lived in the "East House," a pre-existing frame cottage, clapboard painted white, of five rooms with two fireplaces and a veranda on three sides. The East House was also used as a residence for the novitiate order.

Welcomed by Community

The people of Georgia welcomed the Shakers, who by now were widely respected across the country. A favorable article on the order had recently appeared in *Ladies Home Journal,* so the residents of White Oak expected to have good neighbors.

There were no local converts won, but the Shakers made friends in the few years they lived at White Oak. One remembered them as "the best of people and neighbors, scrupulously honest in all their dealings with their fellow man."

There were not enough Shaker hands, however, to make this endeavor a success. Although Georgians thought the Union Village Shakers would move their headquarters to the state, few Believers wanted to go south even though a handsome three-story dwelling was built at White Oak, costing $20,000, with all its modern conveniences. Extravagant compared to traditional Shaker standards, the dwelling was appointed with marble-topped tables, interior plumbing, and kitchens and bathrooms with plenty of carved walnut and polished marble, sporting copper fixtures and raised, marble bathtubs. This same ambitious Union Village leadership had remodeled the modest 1810 Office there into "Marble Hall."

For lack of enthusiasm, the new colony began to fail within the first year. What was worse, large-scale borrowing and mortgaging to finance White Oak created bitter dissension among Shakers back in Union Village. Sold soon after abandonment in 1902, White Oak was acquired by a sportsmen's group, who named it the White Oak Club. It later became a winter estate for successive owners.

Now in private hands, the East House cottage and a barn are all that remain of the White Oak Shaker colony. The original residence and the elegant new dwelling were torn down in the mid-20th century and replaced by modern homes.

Planning Your Visit

The large dwellings occupied by the Shakers at Altama and White Oak were demolished shortly after the middle of this century. Sites of these dwellings and the East House lie hundreds of yards inside privately owned lands and cannot be viewed from public highways.

For further site information contact:

The Georgia Historical Society
501 Whitaker Street
Savannah, Georgia 31401
Tel: 912/651-2128 or 944-2128

Coastal Georgia Historical Society
PO Box 1136
St. Simons Island, Georgia 31522
Tel: 912/638-4666

For lodging/dining information contact:

Camden/Kings Bay Chamber of Commerce
PO Box 130
Kingsland, Georgia 31548
Tel: 912/729-5840

Access to White Oak

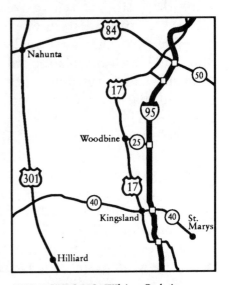

DIRECTIONS: White Oak is about 13 miles west of Brunswick, at the junction of Routes 17 and 252, about the same distance north of the Georgia-Florida line.

From The Shaker Manifesto, April, 1896

[All of our readers will be interested to hear from the dear friends in Florida, who are zealously engaged in that land of flowers in building a religious home. Ed.]

NARCOOSSA, FLA. MAR. 1896.

DEAR SISTER A——:—You are welcome to our home and hearts. How good of you to come and see us in spirit. I hope you may not forget to come often. Now we will step out on the veranda and have a little chat. What do we see? Six large banana trees throwing out their great leaves, four feet long and twenty-one inches wide. From these we may expect a crop the coming year.

The lawn is covered with Bermuda grass. Our flower garden has a sparce sprinkling of verbenas, pinks, lilies and roses, and all these are in bloom. At our right are two strawberry beds, in bearing, and a small patch of sweet potatoes. Just south of this is a pine grove. It is sown to rye and is now beautifully green. Our two milch cows enjoy feeding there some hours, daily. You will observe our pineapple orchard contains not less than 1000 plants. We anticipate a crop some time next year. All our Florida friends who have visited the place say that "the old growers can't beat it." By this we feel quite encouraged. We have a small section for sugar cane, one for cabbages, one for raspberries, and one hundred banana trees in good condition, some may bear fruit next year, others the year following.

Here is a field of Irish potatoes in bloom and by and by we expect a supply of Florida grown Irish potatoes. A section is devoted to the growing of Cassava. It is up and looks well. It is very much like the white yam so largely raised in the West Indies. It is considered good for table use.

Our peach orchard contains 130 trees. Less than one year since, this ground was covered with a grove of tall pines. These have been cut down and their roots taken from the ground

Our garden has a variety of vegetables, and we are now having a supply of radishes, lettuce, greens, etc.

We will now pass into the house. The dining-room occupies a central position. The sleeping apartments are on the west side and a sitting room on the east.

Our room for cooking is so arranged that we do not have the heat and smoke in the dwelling.

We have a well and a pump attached, also a good water tank. As we have no cellar, our milk and various other things share the cool breeze. Our yard is covered largely with Bermuda grass. In the flower beds we have gladiolas, tulips, hyacinths, lantavas and hybiscus. Some of these are in full bloom. We have also in another section orange, plum and persimon trees, twenty-five of each variety.

We have a new barn with sheds attached, also a yard for the hens, and all about these are groves of pine.

We are anticipating a permanent residence at a future date, some two and one half miles distant from our present home, on the shore of Alligator Lake. It is a beautiful place.

Lovingly Your Sister

M.L. REYNOLDS

NARCOOSSEE

"Olive Branch"
Ashton, Florida
1895-1924

An Exit from the North

By the last decade of the 19th century the Shakers had diminished in number as their members grew older and fewer young converts entered the order. Some New York Believers thought it a good step to establish colonies in the temperate South, offering an easier life to Believers than did the northern climate.

In 1894, Shakers from Watervliet, New York came to central Florida's Osceola County in search of land. By 1896, a colony was established on more than 7,000 acres (eleven sections) near the village of Narcoossee, about twenty miles south of Orlando. The members were full of hope as they gave their ambitious new community the spiritual name, "Olive Branch." However, despite hard work and some initial economic success it was closed in 1924.

History of the Site

Much of the tract was lake or swamp, the rest covered with palmetto bush that required massive clearing to be arable. From the start the Believers who came to settle in Florida were not certain the venture was a good idea. They did not have the younger, stronger manpower to carry out the heavy labor required to cultivate the land. It was necessary for them to hire hands and lease oxen to get the work done.

Elder Andrew Barrett who became head of "Olive Branch," wrote home that he considered the task of building a new community that could thrive economically an extremely demanding one. He feared they were forgetting the importance of creating "a spiritual household as well as the temporal." Elder Andrew continued, "to me this was not intended as merely a speculative scheme for a quiet and comfortable home with a good chance to make a few dollars to keep them running." He said, "If God is in it I don't believe he wants any such Business."

Yet the Shakers did make progress at Narcoossee, even though no more than a dozen Believers ever lived there at any one time. In a short time they built a 90 ft. x 60 ft. chicken house, a big barn, a road, which the county finished, and a windmill. They had a cottage built by local carpenters, with two rooms below for the sisters. (They held their service outside on the veranda, since they had no meetinghouse.) Another cottage was built, two lofts high, for brethren. The Sugar Belt Railroad even built a station for the Shakers to ship from. None of this remains.

They were such fine agriculturalists that they succeeded with field crops such as potatoes, sweet potatoes, sugar cane, beans, peas, rice and pumpkins and other crops. They built a successful steam-powered sawmill which could cut 4,000 board feet a day. They began a herd of beef cattle, and worked to develop irrigation and drainage systems. They also had a thriving business in fish, which were abundant in their lakes and streams. Advertisements in the local papers sold their chickens and eggs. Their honey and cane syrup was known as the best in the area.

Fruit trees were planted, and the Shaker gardens were like parks, with flowering bulbs and vines gracing attractive lawns. Most of all, the Narcoossee Shakers were known for

A visitor on the grounds of the Shaker colony in Florida. Original at Osceola County Historical Archive.

their pineapples, even exporting them to Cuba, and developing the finest "pines" in a region known for the very best. Bananas, too, were planted, and began to yield in abundance by 1910. They were still selling in local stores in 1916. Other produce included oranges, peaches, watermelons, strawberries and mulberries.

Highly Respected by Community

In 1908, approaching the high point of the colony, Elder Ezra J. Stewart was hired by the county commissioners to take charge of the county exhibit at the state fair. There he met and befriended the then-famous temperance extremist Carrie Nation, whom he described as reminding him "more of Mother Ann than any woman I have ever met."

Elder Ezra explained Shaker beliefs to her, but said she apparently did not "comprehend the use of celibacy." When he invited her to speak to the Shakers at Narcoossee, she asked, "Can you get me an auditorium? I must have people to speak to." There was no auditorium and so no speech from Miss Nation to the Florida Shakers.

The Shakers were an attraction and well thought of. There were public picnics on their land. (One doctor often sent his patients there for outings.) Such events, plus the opening of St. Cloud in 1909, offered the possibility of converts.

Notoriety

About 1906, the Shakers took in Sadie Marchant, a woman from a nearby sanatorium, who was ill with tuberculosis. She stayed with them for some time. In 1911, during her last days, she talked of suicide, then begged the Shakers to put her out of her misery. Brother Egbert Gillette and Sister Elizabeth Sears twice administered an opiate as a painkiller, and, finally, chloroform, from which the dying woman did not awaken. The authorities investigated and reluctantly arrested the two Shakers, as required by law. Newspapers all over the country reported on the case, virtually all of America being in profound sympathy with the Shakers—the order by now was highly respected.

The *Kissimmee Valley Gazette* voiced admiration for the Shakers, asserting that such an act could only have been committed out of the utmost love: "The Shakers are well regarded as the personification of honesty, uprightness and peacefulness…. Would that Osceola County had ten thousand such people within its border."

The charges against Sister Elizabeth were dropped after a grand jury hearing, and the charges against Brother Egbert after a second. Neither ever went to trial, and the publicity from the episode generated a number of inquiries about joining the Shakers.

However, lack of new converts and the continuing need for a vast effort to clear enough land for more extensive agriculture were discouraging. Nor were the aging sisters and brethren up north eager to resettle in Florida. The Shakers began a series of failed deals to sell over the next few years. All the land was not completely disposed of by as late as 1933. In 1924, the *St. Cloud Tribune* ran a goodbye article as the last Shakers were returning to Mount Lebanon, New York. (Brother Egbert left the order, married, and lived in St. Cloud. When he died in 1945, he was cremated. His ashes remained in the funeral home there until 1990, when they were buried in the cemetery at Hancock, Massachusetts.)

Courtesy Osceola County Historical Society

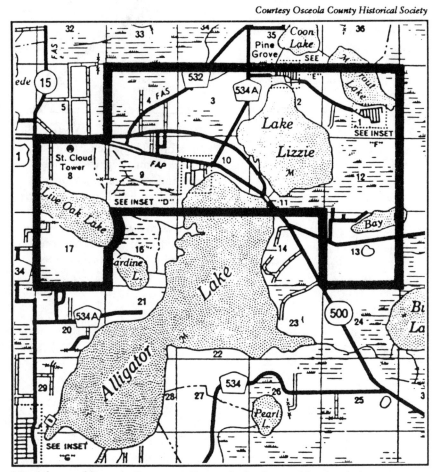

Map of part of Osceola County, outlining the land owned by the Shakers.

Planning Your Visit

The land which the Shakers farmed is now privately owned. Contact the Osceola County Historical Society for site interpretation.

Tourist Information

The Historical Society is open Monday through Saturday 10 a.m.-4 p.m.; Sunday 1-4 p.m. Closed on major holidays.

For further site information contact:

Osceola County Historical Society
PO Box 420552
Kissimmee, Florida 34742
Tel: 407/396-8644

For lodging/dining information contact:

Kissimmee/St. Cloud Convention and Visitors Bureau
1925 East Irlo Bronson Memorial Highway (Route 192)
Kissimmee, Florida
Tel: 407/847-5000

(Lodging Only)
Call 8 a.m.-5:30 p.m.
Tel: 800/333-KISS

Access to Narcoossee

DIRECTIONS: Drive East from St. Cloud on 192. Just east of Route 15 Shaker land begins on your right, and, about 2 miles farther east, on your left. If you take a left onto Pine Grove Road, and go 1-2 miles to Bass Highway, you get a good view of Lake Lizzie, on your right (which the Shakers owned entirely).

SHAKER PUBLIC COLLECTIONS & LIBRARIES

CONNECTICUT

CONNECTICUT STATE LIBRARY
231 Capitol Avenue
Hartford 06115
203/566-4777 or 203/566-5776

Large collection of Enfield, Connecticut, material in special and rare books collection; available only by prior arrangement. Also, a very large collection of imprints, including complete run of Shaker Manifesto.

Hours: Mon.-Fri. 8:30 a.m.-5 p.m.; Sat. 9 a.m.-1 p.m.

ENFIELD HISTORICAL SOCIETY
1294 Enfield Street (Route 5)
Enfield 06082
203/745-1724
(See Enfield, Connecticut chapter for description and hours.)

NEW CANAAN HISTORICAL SOCIETY
13 Oenoke Ridge
New Canaan 06840
203/966-1776
(See New Canaan chapter for description and hours.)

DELAWARE

THE HENRY FRANCIS DU PONT WINTERTHUR MUSEUM AND LIBRARY
Winterthur 19735
302/888-4600

The library division of Winterthur has Edward Deming Andrews Memorial Shaker Collection, rich resource for study of Shakers. Book-length printed guide to collection available. Collection accessible to public. The museum has two rooms featuring Shaker artifacts; open to public as part of museum tour schedule.

Library hours: Mon.-Fri. 8:30 a.m.-4:30 p.m.

Museum hours: Tues.-Sat. noon-5 p.m.
Fee includes self-guided walk in gardens.
Winterthur is 6 miles north of Wilmington, on Route 52.

DISTRICT OF COLUMBIA

LIBRARY OF CONGRESS
Washington 20540
203/566-4777

Books in general collections; special materials in American Folklife Center and Rare Book, Manuscript, and Music divisions.

FLORIDA

OSCEOLA COUNTY
HISTORICAL SOCIETY
840 Bass Road, PO Box 420552
Kissimmee 34742
407/396-8644

(See Narcoossee chapter for description and hours.)

GEORGIA

COASTAL GEORGIA
HISTORICAL SOCIETY
PO Box 1136
St. Simons Island 31522
Tel. 912/638-4666

THE GEORGIA HISTORICAL SOCIETY
501 Whitaker Street
Savannah 31401
912/651-2128 or 944-2128

INDIANA

INDIANA HISTORICAL
SOCIETY LIBRARY
315 West Ohio Street
Indianapolis 46202
Historical Society: 317/233-1882
FAX 317/233-3109
Library: 317/232-1879

The historical society is located conveniently, sharing a building with Indiana State Library and Indiana Commission on Public Records, which are at 140 N. Senate Ave.

Historical Society office hours: Mon.-Fri. 8 a.m.-4 p.m. Though not a major repository of Shaker material, library has a collection of more than three million manuscript items, beginning with colonial settlement. Library also has more than 25,000 books and a picture collection of more than one million items.

Hours: Mon.-Fri. 8 a.m.-4 p.m.; Sat. 8:30 a.m.-4 p.m., Sept. through May. Closed Sat., June through Aug., and during Historical Society's annual and spring conferences.

KENTUCKY

THE FILSON CLUB
HISTORICAL SOCIETY
1310 South Third Sreet
Louisville 40208
502/635-5083
Pleasant Hill material in various departments.

Hours: Mon.-Fri. 9 a.m.-5 p.m.; Sat. 9 a.m.-noon.

KENTUCKY MUSEUM AND LIBRARY
Bowling Green 42101
Museum: 502/745-2592
Library: 502/745-6086.

These are divisions within the Western Kentucky University Department of Library Special Collections and are housed in the

Kentucky Building on the campus, approximately 12 miles east of Shaker Village at South Union.

The library's Manuscripts/Folklife Archives Division contains extensive journals, diaries, business papers, and other materials from the Shakers at South Union, 1800-1916. Other manuscripts include the diary of an 1854 trip made by four leaders of South Union to visit Shaker societies in the East. Patrons required to register prior to using collections. All materials are non-circulating.

Library hours: Mon.-Fri. 8 a.m.-4:30 p.m.; with prior notification, most materials may be used in library reading room Sat. 9 a.m.-4:30 p.m.

The museum has a small collection of artifacts (approximately 40 objects) from South Union, including furniture such as chests of drawers, sewing table, utility table, candlestand, chairs; there are also kerchiefs, boxes, and blankets on display.

Museum hours: Tues.-Sat. 9:30 a.m.-4 p.m.; Sun. 1 p.m.-4:30 p.m. Closed some University holidays.

SHAKER VILLAGE OF PLEASANT HILL
3500 Lexington Road
Harrodsburg 40330
606/734-5411
(See Pleasant Hill chapter for description and hours.)

SHAKERTOWN AT SOUTH UNION
PO Box 30
South Union 42283

502/542-4167
(See South Union chapter for description and hours.)

UNIVERSITY OF KENTUCKY
MARGARET I. KING LIBRARY
Lexington 40506-0039
606/258-8611
Off Rose Street, opposite Columbia Avenue.

Most Shaker materials in Special Collections Division. Appointments with staff specialists are suggested. No copies of Shakertown at Pleasant Hill Collection materials may be made without written permission from President of Shakertown.

Hours: Mon.-Fri. 8 a.m.-4:30 p.m.; Sat. 8 a.m.-noon.

During fall and spring semesters, hours are extended Wed. to 9 p.m. and division is open 2-5 p.m.

MAINE

SHAKER MUSEUM AND LIBRARY
United Society of Shakers
RR 1, Box 640
Poland Spring 04274
207/926-4597
(See Sabbathday Lake chapter for description and hours.)

MASSACHUSETTS

AMERICAN ANTIQUARIAN SOCIETY
185 Salisbury Street
Worcester 01609-1634
508/755-5221

Excellent collection of Shaker imprints and some ancillary materials; manuscript collections not strong.

Hours: Mon.-Fri. 9 a.m.-5 p.m.

ART COMPLEX MUSEUM
PO Box 2814/189 Alden Street
Duxbury 02331
617/934-6634

Shaker furniture collection.

Hours: Wed.-Sun. 1 p.m.-4 p.m., closed holidays.

BERKSHIRE ATHENAEUM
1 Wendell Avenue
Pittsfield 01201
413/499-9486

Public library; much Hancock and other material, including a complete run of the *Shaker Manifesto* and an excellent collection of imprints.

Hours: Sept.-June, open Mon.-Thurs. 10 a.m.-9 p.m.; Fri.-Sat. 10 a.m.-5 p.m.; closed Sun. & holidays. July & Aug, open Mon., Wed. & Fri. 10 a.m.-5 p.m.; Tues. & Thurs. 10 a.m.-9 p.m.; Sat. 10 a.m.-1 p.m.

FRUITLANDS MUSEUMS AND LIBRARY
102 Prospect Hill Road
Harvard 01451
508/456-3924
(See Harvard chapter for description and hours.)

HANCOCK SHAKER VILLAGE
PO Box 898
Pittsfield 01201
413/443-0188
(See Hancock chapter for description and hours.)

MASSACHUSETTS HISTORICAL SOCIETY
1154 Boylston Street
Boston 02215
617/536-1608

Excellent collection of books and pamphlets; few manuscripts.

Hours: Mon.-Fri. 9 a.m.-4:45 p.m.

SHIRLEY HISTORICAL SOCIETY
182 Center Road
PO Box 217
Shirley, 01464
508/425-9328
(See Shirley Chapter for description and hours.)

WILLIAMS COLLEGE, SAWYER LIBRARY
Williamstown 01267
413/597-2568

Part of the Archives and Special Collections Department, this collection is particularly strong in Shaker music and imprints; manuscript material primarily from Mount Lebanon, Hancock & Harvard communities and includes account books and family journals. There is a fine assemblage of spirit messages and early hymnals. Printed material spans 18th-20th centuries.

Hours: Mon.-Fri. 9 a.m.-noon and 1-5 p.m. Appointments required to use Shaker materials.

MICHIGAN

UNIVERSITY OF MICHIGAN
WILLIAM L. CLEMENTS LIBRARY
South University Avenue
Ann Arbor 48109
313/764-2347

Hours: Mon.-Fri. 9 a.m.-5 p.m.

NEW HAMPSHIRE

DARTMOUTH COLLEGE,
BAKER LIBRARY
Hanover 03755
603/646-2037

The library has excellent collection
of books and photographs on
Shaker, and a small collection of
manuscripts. Most photographs
related to Enfield, New Hampshire
Society. There is no one location in
the library where Shaker materials
are kept. Collection open to public,
and hours vary. Those who wish to
consult materials in depth should
write or call in advance. Library on
the north side of college green.

THE HOOD MUSEUM OF ART
Wheelock Street
Hanover 03755
603/646-2808

Collection of Shaker objects.

Hours: Tues.-Sat. 10 a.m.-5 p.m.;
Sun. noon-5 p.m.
No fee.

NEW HAMPSHIRE
HISTORICAL SOCIETY LIBRARY
30 Park Street
Concord 03301
603/225-3381

Good collection of printed sources
from Canterbury and Enfield, New
Hampshire; excellent collection of
New England town histories and
genealogies. More than 50,000
volumes. The Historical Society
Museum collections relate to decorative arts and other state historic
memorabilia, totaling more than
20,000 items. The 1911 museum
building is listed on the National
Register of Historic Places.

Museum & Library Hours:
Mon.-Fri. 9 a.m.-4:30 p.m.;
Sat. noon-4:30 p.m.

SHAKER MUSEUM
SHAKER VILLAGE AT CANTERBURY
East Canterbury 03224
603/783-9511
(See Canterbury chapter for
description and hours.)

MUSEUM AT LOWER
SHAKER VILLAGE
2 Lower Shaker Village
Enfield 03748
603/632-4346
(See Enfield, New Hampshire chapter for description and hours.)

THE SHAKER INN
Box 11, Lower Shaker Village
Enfield 03748
603/632-7800

NEW YORK

AMERICAN SOCIETY FOR PSYCHICAL RESEARCH

5 West 73rd Street
New York City 10023
212/799-5050

Research and lending library has collections of manuscripts, gift drawings, and books, mainly from Watervliet, New York.

Hours: Mon.-Fri. 10 a.m.-6 p.m.

BUFFALO AND ERIE COUNTY PUBLIC LIBRARY

Lafayette Square
Buffalo 14203
716/858-7118

Rare Book Room, Grosvenor Collection; Shaker Collection inventory available for fee.

Hours: Mon.-Fri. 2-5 p.m.

GENESEE COUNTRY MUSEUM

Flint Hill Road, PO Box 310
Mumford 14511
716/538-6822
(See Groveland chapter
for description and hours.)

HAMILTON COLLEGE LIBRARY

Clinton 13323
315/859-4479

Collection of almost 1,000 items, including some manuscripts, photographs and Shaker-related books and pamphlets.

Hours: Open seven days a week when college in session (early September to mid-May), weekdays during summer.

HOFSTRA UNIVERSITY AXINN LIBRARY

1000 Fulton Avenue
Hempstead, Long Island 11550
516/560-5097

Special collections, 9th Floor

Hours: Mon.-Fri. 9 a.m.-5 p.m. and by appointment.

LIVINGSTON COUNTY MUSEUM

30 Center Street
Geneseo 14454
716/243-9147 or 243-2332
(See Groveland chapter
for description and hours.)

METROPOLITAN MUSEUM OF ART

Fifth Avenue and 82nd Street
New York City 10028
212/879-5500

American Wing, Shaker "retiring room" from Mount Lebanon.

Hours: Sun., Tues. & Thurs. 9:30 a.m.-5:15 p.m.; Fri. & Sat. 9:30 a.m.-8:45 p.m.
Fee.

NEW YORK PUBLIC LIBRARY

Fifth Avenue and 42nd Street
New York City 10018-2788
212/930-0801

Special collections, Manuscripts, and Archives Section. Because of the strength of its manuscript materials, the library is a leading center of source material on the Shakers. Book materials in the bibliography and history of the sect are collected comprehensively, and other materials are acquired selectively. The library has original copies of

Joseph Meacham's *A Concise Statement of the Principles of the Only True Church,* as well as extensive archives, including church records, journals, diaries, letters, and personal accounts. Published materials on Shakerism are normally accessed through the General Research Division, room 315; rare books and manuscripts may be consulted with permission from the Office of Special Collections. Appointment recommended.

Hours: Mon., Tues., Wed., Fri. & Sat. 10 a.m.-6 p.m.

NEW YORK STATE LIBRARY
Cultural Education Center,
11th Floor
Empire State Plaza,
Albany 12230
518/474-6282

Extensive collection of Shaker manuscripts has been completely organized and microfilmed and is available in that form from interlibrary loan. Manuscript collection mainly represents Watervliet, New Lebanon, and Groveland, New York, and Harvard, Massachusetts. These include covenants, laws, legal documents, membership and financial records, addresses, biographies, inspired writings, recipes, music, and poetry.

There are also very large collections of Shaker printed materials, including testimonies, monographs, and periodicals such as The Shaker Manifesto. The third major area of resource is the entire Western Reserve collection of Shaker manu-

scripts and printed works on microform, also available for interlibrary loan. A printed "finding aid" to locate Shaker materials is available for a fee.

Hours: Mon.-Fri. 9 a.m.-5 p.m.

NEW YORK STATE MUSEUM
Madison Avenue
Albany 12230
518/474-5353

Collections of furniture, photographs, tools, and products; especially strong in Groveland and Sodus Bay artifacts and archives.

Hours: Daily 10 a.m.-5 p.m.
Appointment necessary.

SHAKER MUSEUM AND LIBRARY
Old Chatham 12136
518/794-9100
(See complete Shaker Museum and Library chapter in main text.)

SYRACUSE UNIVERSITY
GEORGE ARENTS RESEARCH LIBRARY
Syracuse 13210
315/443-2697
Growing library of more than 500 volumes; no manuscripts. Apply to Reader Services librarian.
Hours: Mon.-Fri. 9 a.m.-5 p.m.

NORTH CAROLINA
DUKE UNIVERSITY
WILLIAM R. PERKINS LIBRARY
Durham 27706
919/684-3372
FAX 919/684-2855

The Special Collections Library has six manuscript collections that include Shaker materials; there is also a manuscript collection in the Trent Collection, Medical Center Library, that refers to Shakers. There are also microfilmed records from Pleasant Hill.

University libraries contain approximately 200 books on Shakers, some in the Rare Book Room.

Hours: The Special Collections Library is open weekdays 8 a.m.-5 p.m. and Sat. 1-5 p.m. Hours for the Perkins Library (central library), Divinity School Library, and other constituent libraries vary. Access to Special Collections Library is available upon presentation of proper photographic identification.

OHIO

DAYTON AND MONTGOMERY PUBLIC LIBRARY
215 East 3rd Street
Dayton 45402-2103
513/227-9500

Watervliet, Ohio, community particularly represented in collection; also manuscripts and early publications from various communities. Material covers period of 1808-1983.

Hours: Mon.-Fri. 9 a.m.-9 p.m.; Sat. 9 a.m.-6 p.m.; Sun. 1-5 p.m. during school year. Appointments necessary to use special collection.

DUNHAM TAVERN MUSEUM
6707 Euclid Avenue
Cleveland 44106
216/431-1060

Historic tavern with one room furnished in Shaker.

Hours: Year-round, Sun. & Wed. 1 p.m.-4 p.m. Special tours may be arranged on other days. Fee.

GOLDEN LAMB INN
27 South Broadway
Lebanon 45036
513/932-5065
(See Union Village chapter for description and hours.)

KETTERING-MORAINE MUSEUM
35 Moraine Circle South
Kettering 45439-1927
513/299-2722
(See Watervliet, Ohio chapter for description and hours.)

OHIO HISTORICAL SOCIETY
1982 Velma Avenue
Columbus 43211-2497
614/297-2510
FAX 614/297-2411

The society's Archives/Library Division holds a large collection of manuscript, printed, and audiovisual materials on Shaker. All materials can be used in the library. The society also has a collection of Shaker artifacts.

Hours: Tues.-Sat. 9 a.m.-5 p.m.

OTTERBEIN HOMES
585 North State Route 741
Lebanon 45036
513/932-2020
(See Union Village chapter for description and hours.)

SHAKER HISTORICAL SOCIETY
16740 South Park Blvd.
Shaker Heights 44120
216/921-1201
(See North Union chapter
for description and hours.)

WARREN COUNTY
HISTORICAL SOCIETY
105 S. Broadway
(PO Box 223)
Lebanon 45036
513/932-1817
(See Union Village chapter
for description and hours.)

WESTERN RESERVE HISTORICAL
SOCIETY HISTORY LIBRARY
10825 East Blvd.
Cleveland 44106
216/721-5722

Considered to be the most extensive collection of Shaker books and manuscripts in the world. More than 300,000 pages of manuscript and Shaker printed materials are micropublished as the "Shaker Collection" 1723-1952; and available to researchers. A brochure about this collection is available.

Included in the manuscript section are official documents, journals, testimonies and sermons, inspired writings, music, and photographs. In the 1,300 printed materials are periodicals, books, broadsides, and pamphlets. Considerable numbers of related items from other collections have been microfilmed and added to the Western Reserve collection. The entire microfilmed collection along with ancillary guides and catalog cards is available for purchase.

Hours: Tues.-Sat. 9 a.m.-5 p.m.; closed Mon.
Fee.

PENNSYLVANIA

PHILADELPHIA MUSEUM OF ART
Benjamin Franklin Parkway
Box 7646
19101-7646
215/763-8100
FAX 215/236-4465

Complete Shaker Sister's "retiring room" from Mount Lebanon; other Shaker furniture and artifacts, all part of American Decorative Arts department.
Hours: Tues.-Sun. 10 a.m.-5 p.m.; closed Mon.
Fee, but not Sun. mornings.

VERMONT

SHELBURNE MUSEUM
PO Box 10 05482
802/985-3344

Shaker artifacts are housed in a Shaker shed (expanded in 1850 from an 1834 horse stand) from Canterbury, New Hampshire, and include woodworking and craft tools, household utensils, fire-fighting equipment, baskets, wrought-iron, and furniture.

The museum is a gathering of approximately 40 attractions, including the sidewheel steamboat Ticonderoga, Apothecary Shop, Perennial Garden, Castleton Jail, Covered Bridge, Railroad Locomotive, and a Stagecoach Inn. Also on the site are snack bar, cafeteria, and store.

Disability access: The museum is working to make exhibits and programs accessible to persons with disabilities; a physical accessibility guide and wheelchairs are available at the visitor's center.

Hours: Open year-round; late May-late Oct. daily 10 a.m.-5 p.m.; late Oct.-late May, 90-minute tours of selected buildings offered daily, except holidays, at 1 p.m. Special educational family tours available; reservations suggested.

Museum store hours: daily 10 a.m.-6:30 p.m.; and Sun. noon-5 p.m.

Museum on U.S. Rte. 7, 7 miles south of Burlington.
Fee.

WISCONSIN

MILWAUKEE ART MUSEUM
750 North Lincoln Memorial Drive
Milwaukee 53202
414/224-3200
FAX 414/224-7588

Several examples of Shaker style in extensive and growing collection of American folk art dating from colonial period. Shaker works may be examined by appointment.

Hours: Tues., Wed., Fri.& Sat. 10 a.m.-5 p.m.; Thurs. noon-9 p.m.; Sun. noon-5 p.m. Closed Mon. Disability access: East (lake) entrance.
Fee.

VILLA TERRACE DECORATIVE ARTS MUSEUM
2220 North Terrace Avenue
Villa Terrace 53202
414/271-3656

Hours: Sept.-May, Wed., Sat. & Sun. 1-5 p.m.; June-Aug., Wed.-Sun. 1-5 p.m.
No fee, except for tours, by appointment.

STATE HISTORICAL SOCIETY OF WISCONSIN
816 State Street
Madison 53706
608/262-9576

Hours: Mon.-Thurs. 8 a.m.-9 p.m.; Fri.-Sat. 8 a.m.-5 p.m.

GREAT BRITAIN

THE AMERICAN MUSEUM
CLAVERTON MANOR
Bath, England BA2 7BD

This beautiful nineteenth century estate in southwestern England claims to be "The first American Museum outside the United States," and illustrates 200 years of American history through a series of furnished rooms and exhibits.

One of these rooms is set up in Shaker style, with a peg board along the wall, window framing, a stove, and several pieces of Shaker furniture—most of which was acquired from noted collector and Shaker specialist Edward Deming Andrews.

This exhibit is accompanied by a small display gallery that shows examples of Shaker industries, such as seeds, herbs, boxes and sieves, as well as books and photographs. In the library there are also research books on Shaker life.

Bath has no historical record of Mother Ann having visited, but for those interested in American cultural history, the Shaker Room in this museum is put nicely in perspective with other exhibits of Americana from the seventeenth and eighteenth centuries.

These include the "17th-Century Keeping Room" constructed with beams and floorboards from a house in Massachusetts; an exhibit of quilts, a Conestoga wagon, and an 1830 New England bedroom.

The museum, which opened in 1961, was initiated by two Americans who wanted to increase Anglo-American cultural understanding. It administers an active educational program in cooperation with schools and colleges and is supported by friends from both sides of the Atlantic. The gardens include an American arboretum.

Special exhibits, public lectures, concerts and special functions are presented throughout the year.

Teas and light refreshments, including American cookies, home-made breads and jams, are available; special teas may be booked by parties in advance. Evening parties and suppers can also be arranged.

Hours: The museum is open daily 2-5 p.m., (except Mondays) from March 28-November 1. On Sunday and Monday of Bank Holiday Weekends, hours are 11 a.m.-5 p.m. Gardens are open 1-6 p.m. every day except Monday. Educational tours and special adult tours are arranged year-round by appointment (not in January).

DEFUNCT COLLECTIONS:

MUSEUM OF FINE ARTS
Boston, Massachusetts 02115

SELECTED
BIBLIOGRAPHY

Andrews, Edward Deming. *The People Called Shakers.*
New York: Dover, 1963.

Barker, R. Mildred. *The Sabbathday Lake Shakers.*
Sabbathday Lake, Maine: The Shaker Press, 1985.

Bridge, Ruth, ed. *The Challenge of Change.*
Canaan, New Hampshire: Phoenix Publishing, 1977.

Covington, Dale W. "The East House at White Oak, Georgia."
The Shaker Messenger Fall, 1987: pp. 10-11.

Eastman, Harland H. *Alfred, Maine: The Shakers and the Village.*
Sanford, Maine: Wilson's Printers, 1986.

Emlen, Robert P. *Shaker Village Views.* Hanover, New Hampshire and
London: University Press of New England, 1987.

Grant, Jerry V., and Douglas R. Allen. *Shaker Furniture Makers.*
Hanover, New Hampshire: University Press of New England, 1989.

Kramer, Fran. *Simply Shaker: Groveland and the New York Communities.* Rochester: Rochester Museum of Science Center, 1991.

Lossing, Benson. "A Visit to the Shakers at Mt. Lebanon, N.Y.".
Harper's New Monthly Magazine July, 1857.
(Facsimile reprint, 1978, Shaker Museum Foundation.)

Morse, Flo. *The Shakers and the World's People.*
New York: Dodd, Mead & Co., 1980.

Rose, Milton, and Emily Mason. *Shaker Traditions and Design.*
New York: Crown Publishers, Inc., 1975.

Sears, Clara Endicott. *Gleanings from Old Shaker Journals.*
Boston: Houghton Mifflin Company, 1916.

The Shaker Quarterly. The United Society of Shakers,
Route 1, Box 640, Poland Spring, Maine 04274.

Spence, Richard, and Martha Boice. *Maps of the Shaker West.*
Dayton, Ohio: Western Shaker Study Group, [forthcoming 1994].

Sprigg, June. *By Shaker Hands.* New York: Alfred A. Knopf, 1975.

Stein, Stephen J. *The Shaker Experience in America.*
New Haven: Yale University Press, 1992.

Van Kolken, Diana, ed. *The Shaker Messenger* (Quarterly)
P.O. Box 1645, Holland, Michigan 49422-1645.

Wertkin, Gerard C. *The Four Seasons of Shaker Life.*
New York: Simon & Schuster, Inc., 1986.

White, Anna, and Leila S. Taylor. *Shakerism, Its Meaning and Message.*
Columbus, Press of Fred J. Heer, 1905.

Wisbey, Herbert A., Jr. *The Sodus Shaker Community.* Lyons,
New York: Wayne County Historical Society, 1992.

INDEX

Other Golden Hill Press titles you might enjoy.

HOUSE HISTORIES:
A guide to Tracing the Genealogy of Your Home.
By Sally Light.

Recommended by the American Library Association

This award-winning book explains how to identify the various clues a house may give about its past. Also discussed in detail are the many other possible sources of information — surveys, deeds, wills, censuses, photographs, newspapers, insurance and church records, tax lists, oral interviews, etc. – and how to use them. To help in deciphering such information, an entire chapter deals with reading old handwriting. The book also explains how to apply for a historic register listing and, for those interested in house histories as an occupation, provides several chapters on operating such a business. Doing a house history can be not only fun but rewarding, since it offers the owner, seller or buyer the possibility of increasing the house's value by documenting its origins. A valuable resource for homeowners, preservationists, historians, genealogists, residential real estate brokers and others who deal with old houses.

301 pp., 77+ illustrations, resource section for every state, appendices, glossary, bibliography.
ISBN 0-9614876-1-5. Paperback. $14.95.

HOW TO START YOUR OWN BED & BREAKFAST
A Guide to Hosting Paying Guests in Your House or Apartment.
By Mary Zander.

A critically-acclaimed, comprehensive guide to opening a B&B

Many owners or buyers of older homes, historic or otherwise, have utilized Bed & Breakfast as a pleasant way to raise extra money toward costs of restoration and redecorating. And, if a house has special distinction as being historic or in a historic district and is certified as such by the Department of the Interior, it may qualify for a tax credit or low-cost mortgage if it is being used for a commercial purpose, such as B&B.

201 pp., 27 B&W drawings, resource section for every state, index.
ISBN 0-9614876-0-7. Paperback. $9.95.

HOUSE INSPECTION: A Homebuyer's/Homeowner's Guide
With a Special Section on Older or Historic Homes.
By Ned Depew.

This book helps the homebuyer/homeowner avoid the frustration of making costly or uninformed decisions. Homebuyers can use this guide to spot problems before negotiating price. And, it can help in evaluating how well a house might fit the buyer's needs. Homeowners/homesellers can use the book to survey and evaluate even minor problems which might put off potential buyers. Taking you step by step through a house and its electrical, plumbing, heating/cooling and structural systems, and floor by floor, from basement to attic, the book details what to look for and what to look at. Easy-to-read check sheets are provided for each area of the house, enabling you to quickly note questions and problems and their locations. Further reference to the text and illustrations will suggest what you should be concerned with and its relative expense, what can be ignored, and when you should seek an outside, professional opinion.

210 pp., 25 B&W drawings, glossary, index.
ISBN 0-6914876-4-X. Paperback. $11.95.

Available at your local bookstore or from Golden Hill Press, Inc.,
Box 122 • Spencertown, New York 12165 • 518/392-2358.
When ordering, please add $1.65 postage and handling for the first book
and $.50 for each additional. New York State residents add 7% sales tax.